RETURN AGAIN

THE DYNAMICS OF REINCARNATION

AVRAHAM ARIEH TRUGMAN

DEVORA
PUBLISHING
NEW YORK ◆ JERUSALEM ◆ LONDON

Return Again: The Dynamics of Reincarnation

Published by Devora Publishing Company
Copyright © 2008 by Avraham Arieh Trugman

COVER DESIGN: Benjie Herskowitz
TYPESETTING & BOOK DESIGN: Koren Publishing Services
EDITOR: Abe Weschler
EDITORIAL & PRODUCTION MANAGER: Daniella Barak

Hard Cover ISBN: 978-1-934440-15-5

E-MAIL: sales@devorapublishing.com
WEB SITE: www.devorapublishing.com

Printed in the United States of America

On the first Yahrtzeit of
Reb Meir ben Avraham Yechezkel v'Frayda

May his memory be only for a blessing

In memory of our beloved mothers,
Rosa Belleli & Florence Gelfond
You gave so much to your children and grandchildren
Your love and dedication will never be forgotten
Julie and Larry Gelfond

In honor of our children
Jacob, Hannah & Asher Kark
Rana and Andy Kark

In memory of
Alvin Mintz & Richard & Shirlee Waxler
Gone but never forgotten
We love you today as we have from the start
We'll love you forever with all of our heart
Judie and Alan Mintz

Dedicated to our dear parents
David & Bracha Weinstein
We bless you with long life and good health!
Your loving children: Eliezer, Michal, and Irit

Rabbi Yitzchak Ginsburgh

Gal Einai Institute, P.O. Box 1015, Kfar Chabad 72915, Israel

3 Adar/2, 5768

Dear Avraham Arieh:

Your new book on gilgulim is truly exciting, it is a topic of great public interest, a topic that has intrigued people since the beginning of history.

Of course the purpose of this study as an integral part of the Torah is to inspire us to continually grow in our consciousness and service of God.

The great tzadikim have taught us that in each of our lifetimes on earth we are meant to ascend from level to level, to metamorphize from "gilgul" to "gilgul."

Just before the coming of the Mashiach, in our time, all of the gilgulim of all generations will reach their peak, all souls will be ready to greet the Mashiach with joy and a pure heart.

May your wellsprings, based on the teachings of Chassidut, reach the farthest extremes, and so bring the revelation of Mashiach closer, Amen.

Yitzchak Ginsburgh

Rabbi Zev Leff

Rabbi of Moshav Matityahu
Rosh HaYeshiva—Yeshiva Gedola Matityahu

הרב זאב לף   בס"ד

מרא דאתרא מושב מתתיהו
ראש הישיבה—ישיבה גדולה מתתיהו

D.N. Modiin 71917   Tel: 08–976–1138 טל'   Fax: 08–976–5326 פקס'   71917 ד.נ. מודיעין

Dear Friends,

I have read the manuscript of *Return Again: The Dynamics of Reincarnation* by my friend and colleague, Rabbi Avraham Arieh Trugman, and have found it interesting, informative and enlightening. Although I am not qualified to comment on the Kabbalistic sources, I rely on Rabbi Trugman's record in his past works and on his mentor, Rabbi Yitzchak Ginsburgh, shlita, for the information to be accurate.

This topic is widely discussed and widely misunderstood and distorted. This book will serve as a guide to properly understand these difficult concepts. This will be an aid in realizing how deep, complicated and hidden are the ways of Hashem in this world and how one has to stand in reverent awe of G-d's divine providence of mercy and judgment.

I was especially impressed with the explanation of Rav Sa'adya Gaon's opposition and the differentiation between *gilgul* and *ha'ataka*. As was clearly explained, his opposition was to *ha'ataka* and not *gilgul*, as explained in later Kabbalistic texts.

I recommend this book to all who wish to become acquainted with this concept, as it is presented in a fashion that can be read and studied by all, to gain a proper understanding and appreciation of the Torah perspective of reincarnation.

May Hashem grant Rabbi Trugman and his family life and health and the ability to continue to merit the community with further Torah works.

Sincerely,
With Torah blessings,

Rabbi Zev Leff

CONTENTS

ACKNOWLEDGMENTS

I would like to thank my publisher, Yaacov Peterseil, and editorial and production manager Daniella Barak for their encouragement and advice in preparing this book for publication. Special thanks to my editor, Rabbi Abe Weschler, whose professional and dedicated work helped immeasurably in fine-tuning and improving the original manuscript, all the while making sure my literary voice came through loud and clear.

Special acknowledgment is in order to Rabbi Yitzchak Ginsburgh who provided not only the initial encouragement to undertake this project, but whose insightful tapes and manuscripts on reincarnation were vital to the approach and content of the book. Words cannot express the debt of gratitude I have for all the Torah I have learned from you over thirty years, and even more, the deep friendship between us.

Many thanks to Rabbi Zev Leff, who gave of his time to review this book and write such a beautiful approbation. Your willingness to assist me with all of my books is greatly appreciated and your insight has added much needed guidance.

My deep appreciation to Rabbi Shlomo Carlebach, z"l, for his love and encouragement that still inspire me and give me strength even after all these years.

Many thanks to our dear friends who assisted in the publication of this book through their very generous dedications:

Zvi and Shoshanah Gelt, Alan and Laya Lurie, and Rabbi Joe and Rolinda Schonwald. And to Debra and David Flitter, Eddie and Ahuva Shostack, Alan and Judie Mintz, Andy and Rana Kark, Julie and Larry Gelfond, Eliezer, Michal, and Irit Weinstein, and Julie and Josh Geller-Fine. May your living and departed loved ones receive much merit from all who benefit from this book. Thank you from the depths of my heart.

An exceptional thank you is due to a very special group of women I have been privileged to be learning with these last few years. While I was writing this book I presented a series of twelve classes on reincarnation, which was instrumental in helping me organize my thoughts on the subject in a coherent manner. Your insightful questions and comments helped immensely, and your sincere interest in the material was so encouraging. Therefore I want to thank Fern Allen, Hilorie Baer, Symma Freedman, Rachel Frielich, Chavi Lee, Shirel Levine, Esther Hadasa Lowenthal, Laya Lurie, Ruth Sara Sager, Eliana Schonwald, Rolinda Schonwald, Linda Adams Troy, and Rachel Trugman. Special thanks go to Dr. Heidi Fleiss-Lawrence, who has so graciously and enthusiastically hosted the class. I hope we can continue learning together for many years to come.

All my books are intrinsically connected to the educational work of Ohr Chadash, whose mission is to provide a spiritual, relevant, and meaningful experience of Judaism to the widest possible audience. Although it would be impossible to thank everyone who has generously supported our endeavors, I would like to take this opportunity to thank Marty and Chavi Lee for their generous support from the inception of Ohr Chadash. Our ongoing prayers are for Marty to have a complete and quick *refuah shelema*.

Very special thanks to Barbara and Michael Katch, whose sincere belief in the educational work of Ohr Chadash has allowed us to expand and create new programs and initiatives. May the merit of your partnership with us give you great *nachas* and may our friendship continue to blossom.

Many thanks for generous and ongoing support are due to: Zvi and Shoshanah Gelt, George and Sheera Gumbiner, Andy Siegel, Scott and Sally Alpert, Alan and Laya Lurie, and Rabbi Joe and Rolinda Schonwald. It is deeply appreciated.

And to Chuck and Betty Whiting, Michael and Barbara Schwartz, Daniel and Avia Farber, Jaime and Eitan Rosenthal, Brahm and Lynn Silverstone, Aviva Gottlieb, Rabbi Henoch Dov and Sari Hoffman, Tuvya and Jayne Brandt, Jeffrey and Shelly Cohen, Ivan and Barbara Geller, Walter Goldberg, Nate and Amy Davidovich, Ken and Vickie Pepper, Debra and David Flitter, Marvin Kark, and Andy and Rana Kark, thanks for your ongoing support and vote of confidence.

To my wife Rachel and my children and their families – to you I always return again, for you are my home and the place where my heart resides.

And above all to the *Ribbono shel Olam*, the Master of the World, who continually renews me, never gives up on me, always inspires me, and has graciously given me life again and again....

INTRODUCTION

It is said that whenever a new prospective student would approach the Ba'al Shem Tov, the charismatic founder of the Chassidic movement, he would begin querying the student by asking: "What do you remember?" With this question the Ba'al Shem Tov was already revealing to the student that what he had to teach him was much deeper than just ordinary book knowledge. This question would, according to Rabbi Yitzchak Ginsburgh, stir within the student the hidden levels of his unconscious, touching on the unresolved and repressed problems of this lifetime, as well as awakening deep-rooted memories of previous lifetimes, reaching back to even the most primal memories of the pristine, heavenly state of the student's soul before its descent into a physical body (Yitzchak Ginsburgh, *Transforming Darkness into Light* [Jerusalem: Gal Einai, 2002], pp 123–125).

This same idea was later developed by the Ba'al Shem Tov's great-grandson, Rebbe Nachman of Breslov, in his now classic allegorical story, The Seven Beggars. In this profound yet whimsical tale, two orphan children are lost in a forest. There they are assisted by seven beggars, each one maimed with a seeming physical disability. When the two children later marry each other, these same beggars come and bless the couple to be like them, for in truth their disabilities were not what they seemed at all, but were actually wondrous traits. Each beggar, along with his individual blessing to the couple, also related a tale. The first beggar told of a group of men at sea who decided to amuse each other by recalling their earliest memory. The oldest began by saying, "I remember when they plucked the apple from the tree." They were amazed at how ancient a memory this was. The next, who was younger, said, "I remember when the candle burned." They all agreed that his recollection was even more ancient, even though he was younger. The next, who was younger still, related that he recalled when the fruit first began to form. The next one said he remembered when they brought the seed to plant the fruit. The next remembered the wise men who found the seed. Then another remembered the taste of the fruit before it even entered the fruit. And another remembered the smell of the fruit before it came into the fruit. Then one more remembered the form of the fruit before it penetrated the fruit.

The beggar who was telling the story then said that he, the youngest of the group, told them that he recollected everything that they remembered and, in addition, remembered absolutely nothing. Everyone was amazed that the very youngest had the most primordial recollection of them all.

Writing a book about reincarnation is like asking the question: "What do you remember?" For deeply imbedded in the soul are wisps of primal memories that are as elusive as they are real. As we shall see, every person is rooted in the most pristine of realities, from the physical body that houses the soul, to his or her intellectual, emotional, psychological, and spiritual composition. To contemplate the mysteries of reincarnation is to grapple with the identity, nature, and purpose of not only the individual soul, but all of creation.

Although there are a small number of excellent books in English that discuss reincarnation in the Jewish tradition, I felt that this subject deserved to be placed in a broader context, where its general concepts could be seen to correspond and reflect reality on an astonishing number of levels. In addition, not only the mechanics of how reincarnation works needs to be understood, but its deep and profound underlying principles need to be elucidated in order to appreciate their full implications. The idea of reincarnation in Judaism does not appear in a spiritual or intellectual vacuum; rather it conforms and, in many cases, clarifies many important and fundamental concepts integral to a world view that is Jewish.

For many people it will come as a surprise or even shock that reincarnation is part of the Jewish belief system. This is understandable in that until recently the concept, although an integral part of the ancient Jewish mystical tradition, was largely unknown to wide segments of the Jewish people. Since the recent resurgence in interest in Kabbalah, this and many other teachings of the mystical tradition have been given wider exposure and have gained normative Jewish acceptance.

I myself became very interested in this subject in response to a tragic death with which I was trying to come to terms. The more I delved into not only the true Jewish teachings on reincarnation, but more important, their implications for understanding the soul and its place in the vast sweep of human history, the more I felt these important teachings needed to be understood and integrated into the mindset of a wider audience. I slowly became aware that when properly conceived, these teachings could not but effect a paradigm shift in how we see the world and our place in it.

The development of our subject will unfold in the following manner. We will begin by investigating the roots of reincarnation in the written and oral Torah, and especially in the wisdom of Kabbalah and *Chassidut*, as the teachings of the Chassidic movement are referred to. In addition, we will attempt to explain how historically the belief in reincarnation moved from a relatively hidden doctrine to its more open and revealed status today.

We will then delve into the larger spiritual context where we will demonstrate how reincarnation is consistent with many important and fundamental Jewish beliefs and principles. Based on this foundation we will discuss the implications of reincarnation in terms of a broader Jewish belief system. The result of this exploration of the subject will reveal many new and fascinating ideas regarding not just our immediate topic but also about the purpose of creation, the soul, and its ultimate rectification.

Following these reflections we will explain the actual dynamics of reincarnation as taught in Kabbalah. These ideas need much thought and are actually quite complex. Nonetheless, we will endeavor to present in a simple and organized manner its basic teachings as revealed through the ages, and in particular, as expressed by Rabbi Yitzchak Luria (1534–1572), known as the Arizal, the great teacher and master of Kabbalah of Safed, who, more than any other person, revealed the core principles of reincarnation.

Next we will apply what we have learned to the larger context of human development and history. We will see how these teachings are integral to viewing history as an ongoing spiritual progression, and especially how they are integrated into a belief of the culmination of history in the Messianic era and beyond.

Finally, we will trace a number of historical individuals through their various rebirths, as taught by the Arizal. These revelations are truly fascinating and shed much light on understanding these figures and their actions.

Despite our best intentions to present as full and complete a picture of reincarnation according to Jewish tradition as possible, the truth is that in such a relatively short venue we can but touch on this extremely profound and complex subject. We hope to at least provide a sound basis for its understanding, while those who wish to delve even deeper into this area of thought can make use of the sources quoted throughout the text as a guide through the available literature.

I would be less than honest if I did not conclude this introduction by sharing the following struggle I encountered while deciding to write this book. As I delved deeper and deeper into the source material, not only did my fascination grow but so did a certain fear of not being able to properly transmit the ideas in a manner that could be truly fathomed and accepted by a contemporary reader. For as mentioned above, a real integration of these teachings requires an entire paradigm shift on many levels. Not only did I wonder if I was personally prepared for this, but more so, if I could transmit this wisdom in a way that would do justice to these profound teachings.

Even beyond this, I was confronted with another quandary – how would I be able to transmit this information in a manner that would not be seen by some as too "new age," "occult," or even worse. The reason for this is that for some people the actual mechanics of reincarnation may at first seem outrageous, outlandish, or strain the logical Western mind to the breaking point. How, I asked myself, could I present the material in such a way as to avoid having the average reader discount it all due to some of its more seemingly "eccentric" elements?

When I asked my teacher of over thirty years, Rabbi Yitzchak Ginsburgh, if the time was right for these ideas to be presented in English to a wide and varied audience, he answered that if done properly it was a very worthy endeavor. With that encouragement I decided to stretch my own consciousness in order not only to integrate the material personally, but also to convey these very important ideas to the general public. For according to Rabbi Ginsburgh, a proper comprehension of reincarnation helps the individual greatly in appreciating the various occurrences in his or her own life, and the way in which Divine Providence manifests itself in all matters in this world. As one delves into the study of reincarnation and becomes sensitive to its inner secrets, many facets of one's personality, personal history, and the means of rectifying one's own soul come into an ever sharper focus.

One thought that gave me great comfort was that although some of the ideas related to reincarnation may stretch the logical mind, this is not all that unusual today in comparison with the current teachings of physics and cosmology, whose basic principles are the epitome of paradox, and which at their very core strain the imagination and all semblance of logic. And yet, despite their counterintuitive thrust and the very "strange" and almost unbelievable picture of time, space, and reality they paint, nonetheless these laws of nature and principles have proven to be accurate. It is also true that many of the revelations of modern science are strikingly similar to the teachings of Kabbalah, a very fascinating subject on which much has already been written.

My prayer is that these teachings open new gates of understanding for the reader and shed light on many new pathways of wisdom. Even more, I hope the ideas presented will spark a deep thirst to further pursue the study of these teachings and will have a real and practical effect on each person's personal growth, rectification, and spiritual enlightenment.

CHAPTER ONE:

Reincarnation in Jewish Tradition

$\mathcal{T}$he place to start any investigation into the source of an idea or concept in Judaism is to seek its explicit or alluded to mention in the written Torah – i.e., in the five books of Moses and in the other nineteen books of the Prophets and Writings (altogether comprising the twenty-four books of the Bible, "*Tanach*" in Hebrew), and in the major books of the oral tradition, the Mishnah, Talmud, and Midrash. Further investigation would lead to a study of the cardinal books of Kabbalah, Jewish philosophical and ethical works, and the more modern depository of Chassidic teachings.

As we scan classic Jewish texts, we observe that there are no explicit references to reincarnation either in the written or oral tradition. On the other hand, there are many clear teachings on this subject in the works of Kabbalah and Chassidut. What is more is that this subject is presented in those texts as being based on implicit and hinted-to meanings of many verses and teachings in the written and oral Torah! This seeming discrepancy needs to be addressed first and foremost.

The idea of cardinal tenets of Jewish faith not appearing explicitly in the Bible is not an anomaly. Interestingly enough, many of the major ideas in Judaism are in fact not explicitly mentioned in the written Torah, for the very nature of Torah is quite different from many other "holy" books. The teachings of the written Torah depend entirely on the oral tradition, for in the terse and concise style of the written text is imbedded infinite meaning, nuance, and allusion. Each word, phrase, story, or commandment is to be understood on myriad levels, revealing truths about many different aspects of the human being, the world, and life itself.

For example, belief in the *Mashiach*, "Messiah," and the resurrection of the dead, two of the thirteen principles of faith formulated by Maimonides, are never overtly mentioned in the written Torah. Although the figure of the Mashiach and the era he will inaugurate are the subjects of a significant portion of the prophetic message, they are always couched in hints, allusions, and symbolism.

In another example, the soul's existence, its exact nature and purpose, as well as the belief in an after-life and the eternity of the soul, are issues not clearly defined in the written Torah, whereas these concepts receive prominent attention in the oral tradition.

Even when dealing with the commandments of the written Torah, only a handful of these are presented with their reasons explicitly stated; for the most part, no reasons or explanations are offered for the different Divine decrees. It is in the oral Torah that the ethical, moral, allegorical, and philosophical meanings of these commandments are investigated based on traditions handed down through the generations or through use of principles of exegesis from which meaning is derived from the words and verses in which they are transmitted.

Even those stories or commandments that contain seemingly clear meaning and instruction have been expanded upon in each and every generation, as there is no end to their significance or relevance. Many other fundamental moral and ethical ideas that form the body of Jewish thought have their basis in the written Torah but have only been fully revealed through the oral tradition. Therefore, the fact that reincarnation is not unambiguously mentioned in the Bible is not all that unusual.

The major books of Kabbalah, however, have always taught this idea. In fact, over the last five hundred years these teachings have been expanded greatly. This should not be cause for marvel as the idea that concepts in the Jewish mystical tradition are expanded upon and are revealed to greater degrees over the course of time is an important notion in the overall understanding of the development and accessibility of Kabbalah, especially in our time.

The Kabbalah is an integral part of the Torah and was passed down orally generation to generation in a secret, guarded manner. These teachings are dependent on Divine revelation, and the guardians of these teachings in each generation were granted permission to teach and reveal these secrets according to the level and need of the world at that time. These teachings, according to Kabbalah, are intrinsically connected to the Messianic era, which draws ever closer through the unfolding of history. Therefore, as the Messianic era approaches, the secrets of the Kabbalah become ever more revealed, accessible, and influential.

According to the Talmud, our present six-thousand year cycle of history, which will culminate with the coming of the Mashiach, is divided into three two-thousand year periods. The first two-thousand years are called *tohu*, "chaos," describing the somewhat hectic development of humanity and society as chronicled in the Book of Genesis. The second two-thousand years, the period of Torah, began with Abraham and is based on the formation of the Jewish people, the giving of the Torah at Sinai, and the ongoing attempt of the Jewish people to create a Torah society in the Land of Israel. The third period, in which the Jewish people were scattered throughout the world after the destruction of the Temple, is called the era of the Mashiach, who will lead the world to the climactic apex of history and the culminating purpose of all mankind.

It is significant to note that the initial fundamental texts and teachings of Kabbalah were for the most part either formulated, or compiled and edited, during the beginning of the third period, the era of the Mashiach. It was at this time that the *Sefer Yetzirah*, "The Book of Formation," whose teachings stretch back to Abraham, was edited and made known. The *Bahir*, "Illumination," written by one of the greatest mystics of his generation, Rabbi Nechunia ben Hakaneh, was revealed during this period. Also, at this same time, the mystic teachings of Rabbi Shimon bar Yochai were transmitted to his students, who faithfully handed them down until their compiling and publication in the 1200s during the "golden age" in Spain. This work, known as the *Zohar*, is to this day considered the most primary and influential of all Kabbalistic texts.

The revelation of the *Zohar* took place near the beginning of the sixth millennium – the time which the *Zohar* itself predicted would see an explosion of both secular knowledge and Kabbalistic wisdom. Based on the fact that Noah was six hundred years old at the time of the Flood, the *Zohar* (1:117a) states that in the six-hundredth year of the sixth millennium, the lower waters, symbolizing secular knowledge and technological and scientific advancement, would flood the world. Simultaneously, the gates of the upper waters, symbolizing Torah and Kabbalistic wisdom, would open, flooding the world as well. The sixth century of the sixth millennium in the Jewish calendar corresponds to the century between the years 1740–1840 in the Gregorian calendar. Starting then and extending to our day the world has truly seen an explosion of secular knowledge and technological progress. It is also highly significant that there has been an enormous explosion of interest and study of Kabbalah in our generation. This is true of both the Jewish and non-Jewish worlds.

In both the *Bahir* and the *Zohar*, reincarnation is spoken about openly and explicitly, but it was not until the Arizal that the doctrine of reincarnation was explained so overtly and in such detail. There is no doubt that his teaching the belief in reincarnation served as the turning point in the acceptance and spread of this idea as an authentic part of Jewish tradition. The Arizal himself explained that what allowed him to reveal these mysteries was the fact that as the sixth millennium progressed there was a corresponding expansion of light in the upper spiritual worlds. This then made it possible to begin to reveal these secrets in the lower worlds.

Due to the Arizal's great influence, the concept of reincarnation in Jewish thought slowly became mainstream, until the Ba'al Shem Tov (1698–1760) and the teachings of the Chassidic movement made them even more common knowledge within Judaism. According to Rabbi Yitzchak Ginsburgh, the lights in the upper spiritual worlds began to expand and be revealed below at the time of the Arizal, which in turn accelerated a further expansion of light in the upper worlds. At the time of the Ba'al Shem Tov, these lights began to be revealed in the lower spiritual worlds as well, causing an even greater level of revelation in this world. It is no coincidence that the teachings of the Ba'al Shem Tov correspond to the very beginning of the century predicted by the *Zohar* for major revelations in both the secular and spiritual spheres.

Despite the clear tradition of reincarnation in Kabbalah, there were individuals through the ages who disputed the concept. The greatest of these was Rabbi Sa'adya Gaon (882–942), who directly attacked the idea. In a later chapter we will discuss at greater length why he was opposed to reincarnation and how some of his objections were for legitimate reasons. It has been pointed out that Rabbi Sa'adya did not have access to the teachings of the *Zohar* and had he been privy to Kabbalistic ideas, he might have thought differently. Another major opponent was Rabbi Joseph Albo (1380–1435), who expressed his opposition in his major philosophic work, *Sefer Haikkarim*, a work which was very popular in his day.

Nachmanides (1194–1270), author of one of the greatest of the commentaries on the Torah, was a very important figure in the unbroken chain of Kabbalistic tradition. He points to reincarnation as the key to understanding the deeper meaning of certain biblical verses in a number of places, although he does so in a concealed and metaphoric manner.

Another great figure in history, this time from the age of

the Renaissance, was Don Yitzchak Abarbanel (1437–1508), who served as a close advisor to King Ferdinand and Queen Isabella at the time of the Spanish Inquisition. Unable to rescind the evil decree against the Jews, he personally led the exodus of the Jews out of Spain in 1492. Abarbanel was not involved in the study of Kabbalah, yet he was a great proponent of reincarnation. He is quoted by the Tosafot Yom Tov in the latter's introduction to the important Kabbalistic book, *Emek Hamelech*, that the teachings of reincarnation could be openly discussed as they were not, in his opinion, part of the hidden secrets of the Torah. He further pointed out that even the ancient Greeks, who emphasized logical thought in all matters, believed in reincarnation.

Among Torah scholars in our day there is no opposition to the teachings of reincarnation. Chassidic teachings are replete with references to it, and even the original, primary opponent of the Chassidic movement, the Vilna Gaon (1720–97), who himself authored a number of important Kabbalistic commentaries, acknowledged its existence openly.

One of the most important texts dealing with reincarnation is *Gilgulei Neshamot*, "Reincarnation of Souls," written by Rabbi Menachem Azarya of Fano, a student of Rabbi Yisrael Sarouk, who himself was among the closest students of the Arizal. In his introduction to the book, Rabbi Yerucham Meir Lainer, the son of the Rebbe of Ishbitz, who re-published the book in the 1800's, comments that in this day and age when the teachings of the *Zohar*, the Arizal, and the Ba'al Shem Tov are available to all, there is no longer any reason to fear revealing these teachings to a wider public. On the contrary, there is a great need to reveal them, as a proper appreciation of this subject will be a tremendous aid to understanding many matters relating to one's soul, its ultimate purpose, and its rectification.

An English version of *Gilgulei Neshamot* was published in 2001 in Jerusalem. In the forward written by Rabbi Ezra Batzri, it is explained that due to the popularization of reincarnation in the world in general it was imperative to present the Jewish view of this topic according to authentic Kabbalistic sources. It mentions that he put aside his usual reluctance to endorse a translation of a Kabbalistic text, for in this case, the need to clarify and explain reincarnation according to proper Jewish views was so great.

As an example of how widespread the theme of reincarnation has become, we point to a number of prayers in the Jewish liturgy that make mention of it. In the recitation of the bedtime *Shema*, when an individual expresses his or her desire to forgive and be forgiven for all misdeeds or mistakes of that day in order to go to sleep with a clean slate, the following words are read in the opening paragraph: "Master of the world – I hereby forgive anyone who angered or antagonized me or who sinned against me...whether he did so accidentally, carelessly, or purposely... whether in this incarnation or another incarnation..."

Again, in the additional readings of the *Tashlich* ceremony on Rosh Hashana, when Jews symbolically throw away their sins into a flowing river or other body of natural water, some versions read: "Please, O Merciful and Compassionate King – the soul is Yours, and the body is Your work, have mercy on Your labor. Therefore, let Your mercy be upon us and may we merit the completion of the perfection of our [vital] souls, spirits, and [spiritual] souls...." Other versions read slightly differently: "...may we merit the completion of our [vital] souls, spirits, and [spiritual] souls *in this incarnation...*"

The Song of Songs, written by King Solomon, is read by many immediately preceding the start of Shabbat. In a beautiful prayer recited upon completing the recitation of this profound allegory, the following intention is included: "May the recitation and study of the Song of Songs rise before You, as if we have grasped all the wondrous and awesome secrets that are sealed in it, with all its conditions. And may we be worthy of the place from where spirits and souls are hewn, as if we have done all that is required of us to accomplish – whether in this incarnation or in another incarnation..."

Having briefly reviewed the manner in which the teachings of reincarnation have historically unfolded throughout the ages, we will now return and present more fully some of the verses, stories, and commandments in the Bible where reincarnation is alluded to, as well as a number of important examples of the Kabbalistic sources mentioned above.

REINCARNATION IN THE BIBLE
AND THE ORAL TRADITION

Despite the fact that there are no explicit references to reincarnation in the five books of Moses and the other books of the Bible, there are many hints and allusions in verses or stories that could be interpreted to refer to reincarnation.

One of the first allusions comes at the very beginning of Genesis in describing the birth of Seth: "And Adam knew his wife again and she gave birth to a son and she called his name Seth, 'for God has provided for me another seed in place of Abel, because Cain had killed him'" (4:26). The verse mentions "because Cain killed Abel," a phrase which may initially be taken as superfluous, to indicate that Seth, who was "another seed in place of Abel," according to the Kabbalah, was a reincarnation of Abel whose life was prematurely cut off before he had the chance to complete his earthly mission. The idea of a soul returning to finish a task that was left incomplete forms one of the philosophic bases for this and all subsequent reincarnations. The Arizal, as we will learn in greater depth, put great emphasis on tracing the roots of reincarnation to the very first human beings.

One of the clearest allusions to reincarnation is found in the *mitzvah*, "commandment," of levirate marriage, prescribed in the case of a married man who died prior to fathering children. In such a case, one of the deceased man's brothers would be required to marry the widow in order to "establish offspring for his brother" (Genesis 38:8). The first mention of the application of this law in the Torah is in the case of Onen, who refused to impregnate his brother's wife, Tamar, because he knew that "the seed would not be his" (Genesis 38:9). Nachmanides on this verse explains that this story hides one of the greatest of the Torah's secrets relating to the generations of man. According to Kabbalah he was directly referring to reincarnation of the deceased brother in the son who would be born of the levirate marriage.

A second reference to levirate marriage is in the book of Deuteronomy (25:4–10) where it implies that the son should be named after the deceased brother "so that his name would not be blotted out from Israel." Rabbenu Bachya explains that this is not to be taken literally, as there is no command that the child born from the union bear the deceased brother's name. Rather, it means that the son becomes the spiritual heir to the deceased man's soul, which is understood in Kabbalah to refer to reincarnation.

The Torah portion of *Mishpatim* in the book of Exodus (21:1) begins: "And these are the judgments (*mishpatim*) you shall put before them." This Torah portion, coming right after the section describing the giving of the Torah on Mount Sinai, is among the most important in that it contains fifty-three *mitzvot*, "commandments," an especially large number for one portion. These ordinances form the very basis of Jewish criminal and civil law, and the establishment of a just society.

Discussing the first verse of this portion, quoted above, Rashi cites the Talmudic teaching (*Eruvin* 54b) in which God is described as cautioning Moses not to think that his job would be complete after merely teaching the law to the people two or three times, having them commit it to memory, and then not taking the trouble to make sure that they fathom the philosophy behind the law. Rather, once the people did learn the law, it would be incumbent upon him to educate them concerning the deeper reasons for the laws. This is the intent of the above verse in saying, "before them," he must lay out the full explanation of the law before the people, like a set table prepared for eating.

It is significant that the *Zohar* comments on this very verse that these judgments contain the secret of reincarnation, thus beginning a lengthy and very explicit explanation of the reasons and the manifestations of reincarnation. The obvious implication in the words of the *Zohar* is that the many cases of conflict that arise between people and the various situations of judgment mentioned in this portion of the Torah are connected to accounts not just from the current lifetime of the claimants, but from previous lives as well, and that only now are those old issues being resolved.

The same portion of *Mishpatim* includes the laws concerning premeditated murder and accidental killing: "One who strikes a man who dies will be put to death. But for one who had not waited in ambush and God had caused it to come to his hand, I will provide a place to which he shall flee" (21:12–13). The place to flee is designated as a city of refuge, a place where the unintentional murderer must reside, for he is not deemed totally free from blame. The intriguing question is: What does it mean that God caused it to come into his hand? The obvious inference is that somehow God was acting behind the scenes and had caused this death to occur. The explanation of Rashi is truly remarkable and therefore I will paraphrase his entire comment:

> Why did this event come out from before God? This is what King David said: "As the parable of the ancients says – "from evil ones comes evil" (1 Samuel 24:13). And the ancient parable refers to the Torah, which is the parable of God, Who is the Ancient One of the world. But where does it say in the Torah that "from evil ones comes evil?" It is implied in the words "and God had caused it to come to his hand." And what is this verse speaking about?
>
> This case is about two men. One man had killed accidentally and the other man killed purposely, and there were no witnesses to either act. Therefore, the one who killed premeditatedly was not sentenced to death and the other did not have to flee to a city of refuge. What did God do? He arranged that both men would

come to the same inn. The one who killed purposely sat
under a ladder, while the man who killed accidentally
climbed up on the ladder and fell down onto the one
who killed on purpose, thereby killing him. This time,
though, there were witnesses and so the one who fell off
the ladder had to go to a city of refuge. Therefore, the
one who killed by accident was exiled and the one who
killed on purpose was killed (*Makkot* 10b).

Before discussing the verse with Rashi's explanation, we turn
to another verse and another of Rashi's comments. "When you
build a new house you will make a fence for your roof, so that
you will not place blood on your house if a fallen one falls from
it" (Deuteronomy 22:8). In answering the perplexing language of
"if a fallen one falls from it," Rashi states that he is called a "fallen
one" in that it is fitting (i.e., deserving or destined) that he will
fall. He continues by saying, "nevertheless, don't let his death be
by your hand, for meritorious acts are brought about through the
agency of good people and bad things are brought about through
the agency of bad people." What is so intriguing about Rashi's
explanation here is that twice, when saying "are brought about,"
he makes use of a Hebrew word which shares the same root as the
Hebrew for "reincarnation." (In Chapter Two we will analyze the
various meanings of the Hebrew word for reincarnation.)

Now certainly, both Rashi's comments, as well as the verses
which they attempt to clarify, can be understood as highlighting
the way God apportions justice in the world within one lifetime,
yet they are eerily reminiscent of the dynamics of reincarnation.
These ideas will be developed later and form a good part of this
book. Here we merely point out the allusions in the texts – the
example of the two men at the inn occurs in Rashi's comments to
Mishpatim, the same portion that the *Zohar* explains as referring
to the secrets of reincarnation, while the second example of the
"fallen one" has Rashi using a word that is etymologically related
to the word for reincarnation twice. It is true that Rashi is not known

to have expressed a stance on reincarnation either way, but the sources and words he uses in these two instances certainly allude to it, whether he intended to or not.

This point of "whether he intended to or not" calls for a greater explanation. A general principle as taught by Rabbi Yitzchak Ginsburgh is that if a work is written with *ruach hakodesh*, "Divine inspiration," the writer is not always fully aware of the depths of the various secrets and implications of his words, both of which may only be revealed in later generations. This principle was earlier stated by Rebbe Natan, the primary student of Rebbe Nachman of Breslov. When asked whether novel insights found by a later wise person in statements made by sages in the Talmud were actually known to the sage making the original statement, he replied that they were not necessarily known. But since they were originally stated with Divine inspiration they incorporate future insights and teachings enunciated by wise and righteous people (*The Breslov Haggadah* [Jerusalem: Breslov Research Institute, 1989], Appendix B). Similarly, Rabbi Yehuda Aryeh Leib of Ger, in his monumental work, *Sefat Emet*, writes that it is known that a man can say or write great things, but he himself may not realize the full extent of their profound depths.

We return now to further examples of allusions to reincarnation. When Moses blesses the people before he dies he blesses Reuben "to live and not die" (Deuteronomy 33:6). Rabbenu Bachya explains that this means he should live in the World to Come and not have to return to a body to die a second death. He then goes on to connect this idea to the resurrection of the dead, a subject we will delve into further on.

Every Shabbat we read the following verse: "The Torah of God is perfect, restoring the soul" (Psalms 19:8). The Arizal explains this verse to mean that God restores the soul through reincarnation until it achieves perfection through the fulfillment of the Torah. Another important verse, in a similar vein, states that "…neither does God take away life but devises means that none is lost to Him" (2 Samuel 14:14). Here again the verse is understood to relate to the purpose of reincarnation – that no soul should be lost. For if in one lifetime one does not accomplish his or her purpose or rectification, all is not lost, for the soul is given another chance through reincarnation.

According to Kabbalistic interpretation many of the cardinal allusions to reincarnation are ironically contained in Ecclesiastes, a book which, on the surface of it, would seem to give off the impression that life is only lived once. For example: "One generation passes away and another comes…" (1:4) is interpreted in the *Zohar* and by the Arizal (*Gate of Reincarnations* 8) to mean that the same generation that passes will come again in order to fix itself. And again, "The sun also rises and the sun goes down, and hastens to the place where it rises again" (1:5) is interpreted to relate to both the cycle of nature and to the cycle of reincarnating souls.

Further, Ecclesiastes opens with: "'Vanity of vanities,' says Kohelet, 'vanity of vanities, all is vanity.'" The Hebrew for "vanity" is *hevel*, and hevel is the way to pronounce "Abel" in Hebrew. The Arizal put great emphasis on how all souls find their ultimate root in Adam, Cain, Abel, and Seth. In this light, the "vanity" can be understood as reflecting humanity's inability to fully rectify the original blemishes of these archetypal souls, leading to their being reborn over and over again in each and every generation.

Rabbi Ginsburgh points out that the first letter of *Kohelet*, the Hebrew name for Ecclesiastes, corresponds to the first letter in Cain's name ("*Kayin*"). The next two letters of *Kohelet* are the first and last letters of Hevel, while the last letter of *Kohelet* is the last letter in Seth's name ("*Shet*"). In other words, "*Kohelet*" contains letters from the names of the three sons of Adam, the archetypal souls of all reincarnations.

The final verses of Ecclesiastes are: "The end of the matter, when all is said and done: fear God and keep His commandments, for that is all of man. For God will bring every work into judgment, with every secret thing, whether it be good or whether it be evil."

The first letter of the word "end" in the first verse is a *samech* and it is written larger than the letters around it. The shape of the samech (ס) is a circle and, at the level of souls, symbolizes the wheel or cycle of reincarnation, which will only end when all of the commandments are ultimately fulfilled. Until this occurs the soul is returned in judgment, as stated in the second verse.

In the book of Job, Job's friends come to comfort him after a series of personal calamities. Yet their lack of sensitivity and true understanding of the nature of suffering have the exact opposite effect on him, leaving him more vexed than ever. Then Elihu, the son of Barachel, the youngest of them all, explains suffering in a way that Job can accept. Additionally, he rebukes the others for their lack of understanding. According to Nachmanides he was able to do this as only he understood the secret of reincarnation and its connection to suffering. This is why it is not surprising that perhaps the most important of all verses relating to reincarnation is spoken by Elihu: "Therefore God does all these things twice or three times with a man, to return his soul from the pit, to be enlightened with the light of the living" (33:29). As we will see in Chapter Four, the Arizal sees in this verse an explanation for how reincarnation occurs.

It is also very interesting to note that the name Elihu ben [son of] Barachel equals 358, the numerical equivalent of "Mashiach," who will reveal all the secrets of the Torah and in whose time all souls will begin to reach their full rectification, culminating in the resurrection of the dead.

The above are just some of the verses which contain allusions to reincarnation in the Bible. Many of its stories and characters can be perceived in a whole new light by understanding reincarnation. The Arizal did in fact reveal a deeper comprehension of the texts by tracing the reincarnations of many of the major personalities in the Bible and Talmud. We will delve into some of these examples in Chapter Six.

In the same way that there are no explicit mentions of reincarnation in the Bible, but there are many hints and allusions, so too in the Mishnah, Talmud, and Midrash. One of the most important is the statement, "Phineas – this is Elijah [the Prophet]" (*Pirkei Derabbi Eliezer* 46). Although these two figures lived more than five hundred years apart, those who did not accept reincarnation claimed that the Midrash was talking about one and the same person who had two names and who lived for a very long time. Those who did accept reincarnation felt that this statement is more reasonably explained as an implicit reference to reincarnation. (See the article: "Classical Views of Reincarnation," *Ascent Quarterly*, summer 1998, p. 6.) In Chapter Six we will discuss the soul of Phineas and its connection to Elijah.

"The sun also rises and the sun goes down, and hastens to the place where it rises again" (Ecclesiastes 1:5) is used by the Talmud to describe the phenomenon of one great sage being born on the same day that another great sage passed away. "When Rabbi Akiba died, Rebbe [Judah the Prince] was born. When Rebbe died, Rav Yehuda was born. When Rav Yehuda died, Rava was born. When Rava died, Rav Ashi was born. This is to teach us that a *tzaddik* does not leave this world *until another tzaddik like him* is born, as it is said: "The sun also rises and the sun goes down, and hastens to the place where it rises again" (*Kiddushin* 72b). In the Kabbalah, this passage is explained as referring to reincarnation.

The Arizal, in discussing this passage, said that the four sages mentioned were all in fact reincarnations of Rabbi Akiba. Before Rebbe compiled the Mishnah, the very first codification of the oral tradition, it was Rabbi Akiba who was the main link in the unbroken chain of transmission of that tradition all the way back to Mount Sinai. Later, Rav Yehuda and Rava were very important links in the ongoing discussions of the Mishnah, which were finally redacted by Rav Ashi in the monumental work known as the Talmud. These five sages were all in essence one soul and they each made a critical contribution to the development of the

Mishnah and the Talmud, the foundation of the oral tradition down to our own day.

Another important reference to reincarnation according to Kabbalah is the account of the ten martyrs who were tortured to death during the time of the Roman persecutions. This story is included in the prayers of Yom Kippur and on the fast day of Tisha Be'Av. The excuse the Romans offered for torturing the ten sages was that the brothers who had sold Joseph were never punished. In the description of this incident as it appears in the prayers of Yom Kippur, the Roman ruler Lulianus concocts his plan for torturing the sages after reading in the portion of *Mishpatim* that one who kidnaps another and then sells him is liable to the death penalty (Exodus 21:6). When the sages admitted that the penalty for kidnapping and selling an individual was indeed death, Lulianus condemned them to die in place of the brothers of Joseph. The sages requested three days in order to determine if this decree was from God. Rabbi Ishmael pronounced one of God's secret names and was transported to heaven where the angel Gabriel revealed to him that this was truly their destiny.

It is fascinating that the portion (*Mishpatim*) in which Lulianus found his pretext upon which to base his execution of the sages, is the same portion the *Zohar* explains as containing the secrets of reincarnation, as we mentioned above. According to one statement, the Arizal did indeed consider the ten martyrs to be Joseph's brothers reincarnated, and viewed their deaths as an atonement for the sale of their brother.

The ten martyrs were killed right before and after the destruction of the Second Temple, which according to the Talmud was destroyed for baseless hatred, a malady that began with the sale of Joseph. The Arizal taught that the arousal of all Jewish souls in the future to repent and come close to God and Torah is a result of the martyrdom of these ten Torah giants. Among the ten was Rabbi Akiba, whose death while saying the Shema became a source of strength and inspiration for future generations. On the very day he died, Rebbe was born, insuring the continuity of Torah for all times.

The Talmudic tractate *Niddah* (30b) records a discussion concerning the oath the soul is required to make, to be righteous and not evil, before it can be born. The proof text offered is from Isaiah (45:23): "Because to Me will every knee bend and every tongue will swear..." The Talmud interprets "Because to Me every knee will bend" as referring to the day of death, and "every tongue will swear" as the day of birth. Maharsha, Rabbi Shemuel Eidels, a great Talmudic commentator, asks the obvious question: Why does the verse mention the day of death before the day of birth? The answer, he writes, lies in the secret of reincarnation. He goes on to explain that even though all souls swore at Sinai to accept the Torah, individuals are asked to swear once again to be righteous and not to do evil, as they had in their previous incarnation.

In discussing the statement in *Pirkei Avot* (4:11), "Ethics of the Fathers," "whoever fulfills the Torah despite poverty will ultimately fulfill it in wealth," Rebbe Nachman of Breslov declares that this is alluding to the secret of reincarnation (*Likutei Moharan # 200*).

In Deuteronomy, when Moses is preparing the people to continue without his leadership, he gathers them together and states the following words: "Neither with you alone do I make this covenant and this oath, but with him who stands here with us today before God our God, and also with him that is not here with us today..." (29:13). The straightforward explanation of this verse is that the covenant is being made not only with that generation, but with all future generations as well. The deeper meaning is that the future soul of every Jew, and even all those who would one day convert and join the Jewish people, were present at the giving of the Torah at Sinai, and it is this covenant that Moses is renewing with the new generation about to enter the Land of Israel.

Similar to how a proper understanding of reincarnation sheds new light on many verses and stories in the Bible, so too with the study of the Mishnah, Talmud, and Midrash. The above are but a few of the many hints and allusions to reincarnation in these holy texts. Delving deeply into the matter of reincarnation reveals a whole new level of understanding not only of the Jewish texts, but of their profound relevance for our lives as well.

KABBALISTIC SOURCES

Whereas references to reincarnation in the texts mentioned above are all hidden in layers of metaphor and allegory, this is not the case in Kabbalistic texts. It is in these writings, handed down and studied by some of the greatest minds and holiest souls of each generation that the concept of reincarnation is expounded.

We begin our overview with the *Bahir*. Attributed to Rabbi Nechunia ben Hakaneh, a revered first century sage, it is one of the most ancient of Kabbalistic texts. In this relatively short but highly influential book, reincarnation is mentioned a number of times. Some of the references relate to the verse in Ecclesiastes (1:4): "A generation goes and a generation comes...," discussed in the previous section of this book. The *Bahir* (121, 122, and 155) clearly understands this verse as referring to reincarnation. In two other longer passages (184 and 185) the *Bahir* explains in parable form how reincarnation is bound up with the ultimate coming of the Mashiach, an important subject we will develop further on. Perhaps the most important statements in the *Bahir* (194 and 195) regarding reincarnation tie it to an understanding of Divine justice and the very troubling question of why the righteous suffer:

> Why is there a righteous person who has good, and [another] righteous person who has evil? This is because the [second] righteous person was wicked previously, and is now being punished. Is one then punished for his childhood deeds? Did not Rabbi Simon say that in the Tribunal on high, no punishment is meted out until one is twenty years or older. He said: I am not speaking of his present lifetime. I am speaking about what he has already been, previously. His colleagues said to him:

How long will you conceal your words? He replied: Go out and see. What is this like? A person planted a vineyard and hoped to grow grapes, but instead, sour grapes grew. He saw that his planting and harvest were not successful so he tore it out. He cleaned out the sour grape vines and planted again. When he saw that his planting was not successful he tore it up and planted it again. How many times? He said to them: For a thousand generations. It is thus written (Psalms 105:8), "The word that He commanded for a thousand generations" (*Bahir*, trans. Aryeh Kaplan [York Beach, Maine: Samuel Weiser, Inc., 1979], p. 77).

The *Zohar* and the *Tikkunei Zohar*, the foundation texts of Kabbalah, mention reincarnation in scores of places. There is no doubt that the Arizal based much of his system of reincarnation on traditions already taught in the *Zohar*. It is said of the Arizal that through Divine inspiration he was able to extract from the *Zohar* the meaning of its most profound secrets. Therefore many of the sources in the *Zohar* we now present were taken by the Arizal and explained in great detail, as will be seen in the continuation of the book. The following is a very general summation of some of these sources and the contexts in which reincarnation is mentioned.

We already highlighted earlier the *Zohar's* explanation of the first verse of the portion of *Mishpatim* as containing the secrets of reincarnation: "These are the judgments (*mishpatim*) you shall put before them" (*Zohar* 2:94a). The *Zohar* continues to discuss this theme for many pages.

The verse already quoted by us – "Therefore God does all these things twice or three times with a man, to return his soul from the pit, to be enlightened with the light of the living" (Job 33:29) – is explained by the *Zohar* to mean that God gives a person two or three opportunities through reincarnation to make some movement towards rectifying his sins and errors. If there is no movement whatsoever, then the soul is not given any further chances. If on the other hand the soul makes even some slight improvement, then he is given up to even a thousand opportunities, as it says, "The word that He commanded for a thousand generations."

"One generation passes away and another comes...," is another verse often quoted by the *Zohar*, and also cited earlier as well. These verses, together with the various other teachings in the *Zohar*, became important foundation stones for what the Arizal had to say on this subject.

One such teaching from the *Zohar* is the parallel seen between the three opportunities for the soul to return in a body and the three colors surrounding the pupil of the eye, each color representing a different opportunity. The pupil in the center then represents the soul, and all four elements together symbolize the integral unity and wholeness of the component parts (*Tikkunei Zohar* 6:22b).

The mitzvah of levirate marriage, discussed above, is clarified in terms of reincarnation (*Zohar* 2:100a, *Tikkunei Zohar* 21:56a; 26:72a). In addition, it is stated that anyone leaving this world without having children causes the soul to return once again to a body (*Zohar* 3:216a; 1:186b).

An underlying reason offered for why a soul would need to return to this world is its inability to do *teshuva*, which means to repent, or draw close to God and the pure and holy root of his or her own soul essence (*Tikkunei Zohar* 32:76b; 69:103a; 70:126a). The soul is given many chances, even a thousand, as long as it shows signs of progress towards real rectification. If true and sincere teshuva occurs then the need for reincarnation is reduced. The perplexing reality of the righteous suffering can now be explained simply that the individual, while righteous in his present incarnation, must make good on debts that he owes from previous lifetimes (*Tikkunei Zohar* 70:133a/b).

Reincarnation is connected to the concept of the resurrection of the dead in a number of places, such as when dealing with the complex question of which bodies will actually be resurrected.

It also comes up in the discussions relating to how bodies will "roll" (or tunnel) underground to the Land of Israel where the resurrection of the dead will occur. The root verb for "roll" is significantly identical to the root for reincarnation (*Zohar* 1:131a; 2:105b; *Tikkunei Zohar* 40:81a). In Jewish tradition the resurrection of the dead is seen as the final climactic event in the Messianic process. In the *Zohar*, as well as the Talmud, the tradition is cited that the Mashiach will not come till all the souls leave the "body," the name of the heavenly repository of all souls that ultimately will need to be in this world in order for him to be revealed (*Zohar* 1:119a; *Avodah Zarah* 5a; *Yevamot* 62a; *Niddah* 13b). The connection between reincarnation, the Mashiach, and the resurrection of the dead is another subject we will be delving into more thoroughly in later chapters.

Many other verses, mitzvot, stories, or biblical characters are explained with reference to reincarnation. Whether a person can reincarnate into other forms such as animals is discussed and affirmed (*Tikkunei Zohar* 70:133a). This is an area needing much clarification and the Arizal discusses it at length.

The mitzvah of sending away the mother bird before taking her eggs (Deuteronomy 21:6–7) is among the most mysterious of Divine decrees and is treated in all commentaries as containing very deep secrets. The *Zohar* in one place explains it as a Divine allegory about reincarnation (*Tikkunei Zohar* 6:23b).

According to Jewish law a body must be buried as soon as reasonably possible. In Jerusalem the custom is to bury even at night so that a body will not remain in the city unburied overnight. The *Zohar* explains the spiritual reason for this to be that as long as the body is not buried, the departed soul remains in limbo and cannot be elevated and purified, or if deemed necessary, reincarnate and enter another body (*Zohar* 2:88b).

A very important concept mentioned briefly in the *Zohar* and explained at great length by the Arizal is that of *ibbur*, "impregnation," where a soul from the upper worlds enters into a person in this world for a limited time in order to assist that soul or to be assisted itself (69:100b). This is yet another complex and profound concept that will be revisited in later sections of this book.

We have also already discussed the matter of the ten martyrs, which is seen by the *Zohar* to connect to the ten sons of Jacob who sold their brother (*Tikkunei Zohar* 69:103a). Additionally, the *Tikkunei Zohar* discusses other figures in similar terms: Cain, Abel, and Seth (69:100b; 69:114b; 69:115a); Moses and his father-in-law Jethro (69:100b); Phineas, who saved Israel from a plague (Numbers 25:1–9; *Zohar* 3:215–216); and the souls of Nadab and Abihu, the sons of Aaron, who died when bringing an unauthorized fire offering into the Tabernacle (Leviticus 10:1–4).

All of these examples are some of the many references made to reincarnation throughout the *Zohar*. The fact that there are so many, and that they are so explicit, makes the *Zohar* the basis for all subsequent teachings regarding this topic in Jewish tradition. Despite the open treatment of the subject in this basic text of Kabbalah, it remained a relatively secret concept until the Arizal and the Ba'al Shem Tov brought it into mainstream Jewish thought.

After years of learning the very depths of the Jewish mystic tradition, the Arizal was instructed by Elijah the Prophet, from whom he received much of his wisdom, to go to Safed in order that he could make known all that was revealed to him. Although he spent slightly less than three years in Safed and died at the very early age of thirty-eight, the impact his teachings had on not only Kabbalah, but Jewish thought in general, is astounding. The primary student of the Arizal, Rabbi Chaim Vital, spent nearly twenty years after his teacher's death compiling, editing, and organizing his master's teachings. When they were finally published they became, along with the *Zohar*, the fundamental texts on which all subsequent Kabbalah is based.

The works containing the teachings of the Arizal, known as *Kitvei Ha'ari*, are organized into eight gates or sections, and they cover a wide range of subjects, all revealing incredible depths of mystical understanding. In illuminating the secrets of the Bible and the various texts of the oral tradition, new insights are revealed, as well as a groundbreaking system of meditation and deep intent in prayer. The writings of the Arizal present a complex and highly revealing view of cosmology that parallel to a great degree many of the discoveries of modern physics. In addition, he revealed a new understanding of the spiritual worlds and their organization, along with a holistic view of the nature of the soul, its powers, and its means of expression.

One of the eight gates is devoted exclusively to the subject of reincarnation, which gives us a sense of how important this idea was in his overall system. Throughout our book, but especially in Chapter Four, we will return again and again to his teachings. Subsequent to the extensive treatment given to this subject by the Arizal, and due to the enormous respect by all segments of Jewry for his teachings, the implications of reincarnation in understanding Torah texts, the world we live in, and its relevance to each and every individual, became far more persuasive.

There is no doubt, though, that the key figure in the spread of these ideas to the masses and not just to Torah scholars was the Ba'al Shem Tov. Whereas the Arizal was essentially a very private person who spent much of his life in relative isolation and imparted his teachings to a very small group of committed students, the Ba'al Shem Tov believed that the time had come to open these teachings up to the widest audience possible, and in so doing, revolutionized the accessibility of Kabbalah. Woven into the very fabric of Chassidic ritual, custom, learning, and worldview are the mystical teachings of Torah.

Another very important figure in explaining Kabbalistic ideas in a clear and simple form was Ramchal, Rabbi Moshe Chaim Luzzato (1707–1746). He took the entire oral and Kabbalistic tradition and created a unified philosophical system of deep mystical concepts combined with Jewish values and ethics. His two classic works studied by all segments of Jewry to this day are *Derech Hashem*, "The Way of God," and *Mesillat Yesharim*, "The Path of the Just."

In the section of *Derech Hashem* explaining Divine Providence, Ramchal includes a section on reincarnation (Part 2, 3:10). Due to its brevity, yet simple clarity, we include here the entire section:

> There is another important principle regarding God's providence. God arranged matters so that man's chances of achieving ultimate salvation should be maximized. A single soul can be reincarnated a number of times in different bodies, and in this manner, it can rectify the damage done in previous incarnations. Similarly, it can also achieve perfection that was not attained in its previous incarnations. The soul is then ultimately judged at the end of all these incarnations. Its judgment will depend on everything that took place in all its incarnations, as well as its status as an individual in each one.
>
> When an individual has a reincarnated soul, it is possible that he will be affected in a particular manner as a result of his deeds in a previous incarnation. The situation in which he is placed may follow from this, and this situation may bring with it the special responsibility given to him, as discussed earlier. God's judgment of each individual is extremely precise, depending on every aspect of his nature and including every detail of his exact situation. But in the Future World, which is the true good, no individual is required to sustain a liability which is not the result of his own doing, but a result of his mission and responsibility in this world, as parceled out by the Highest Wisdom. In cases such as these, the individual is judged accordingly.
>
> There are many details in the concept of reincarnation, involving the manner in which an

individual is judged according to one incarnation, and how this judgment depends on previous incarnations. The crucial point, however, is the fact that all is truly fair and just as the Torah states (Deuteronomy 32:7), "The Creator's work is perfect, all His ways are justice." No created thing can encompass God's thoughts or the profound depth of His plan. We only know that, like all other concepts, the principle of reincarnation as one of man's experiences also follows the rule of fair judgment, as decreed by God to perfect mankind in general (Moshe Chaim Luzzatto, *The Way of God*, trans. Aryeh Kaplan [Jerusalem, NY: Feldheim Publishers, 1977], pp 125–126).

With this short but highly articulate description of reincarnation we have completed our brief overview of the alluded to, as well as the explicit sources of reincarnation in Jewish texts. We now turn to the larger context in which the idea of reincarnation is taught, in order to better understand its place in the Divine scheme.

CHAPTER TWO:

Reincarnation in a Broader Context

No concept or idea can be understood in a vacuum, divorced from a broader context, whether that context be the natural world and the laws of the universe, or whether it be a historical, cultural, religious, or spiritual framework. Reincarnation is no exception. Its main principles, as we shall see, are in tune with many cardinal Jewish beliefs and correspond to numerous levels of reality.

The words for "nature" and "ring" in Hebrew, *teva* and *taba'at*, are homiletically related through the concept of rings, circles, and cycles. The cycles of nature are all around us and we experience them continually. From the rising and the setting of the sun each day to the recurrent phases of the moon each month, from the rising and the ebbing of the tides to the ever-changing seasons, we live within the reality of the constant motion of the cycles of nature.

A Torah lifestyle emphasizes living within the context of nature in a myriad of ways. The three daily prayers are aligned with morning, afternoon, and evening. The celebration of the weekly Shabbat and the consecration of the new moon alert us to the renewal of time. The flow of the holidays and their intimate connection to both agricultural processes and the calendar, tie us to the cycle of the seasons and the solar year. The observance of the Sabbatical year connects us to an even larger cycle of the passing of time, as does the marking of every fiftieth year as a Jubilee year. The tradition that this cycle of history will culminate in the Messianic era in the seventh millennium binds us to an even grander concept of cycles and time.

Reincarnation is based on cycles as well. The word in Hebrew for reincarnation is *gilgul*, a word which comes from the root *galol*, "to roll," and is built on the base of the words, *gal*, "wave," and *galgal*, meaning "circle" or "wheel." Thus gilgul implies the recurring cycle of life and death, and the continual process of growth and rebirth of the soul.

In Ezekiel's vision of the chariot, the most explicitly mystical section in the Bible, two fundamental concepts in Kabbalah are mentioned that are quite relevant to reincarnation. The first is found in the verse describing certain angels he perceived: "And the living creatures ran and returned like the appearance of a flash of lightning" (Ezekiel 1:14). The idea of "run and return" is employed by Kabbalah and Chassidut to describe the basic dynamic of all creation, from the rhythmic beat of the heart to the waxing and waning of the moon, to the inward and outward motion of breath, to the dynamic energy of the atom. All of nature and life is running and returning, ebbing and flowing, dying and being reborn anew.

The second important idea in the vision of the chariot is the constant references to wheels. For example: "The appearance of the wheels and their work was like the color of an emerald, and the four [faces] had one likeness, and their appearance and their work was as it were a wheel in the middle of a wheel" (ibid 1:16). The image of a wheel within a wheel reminds us of the double language of gilgul, also a double wheel. Similarly, reincarnation implies elements of a previous life enclothed within a current life, coexisting and operating toward the rectification of the soul.

The concept of "enclothment" is a major one in Kabbalah in general, and in the teachings of the Arizal in particular, while its application is at all levels of existence. The ultimate level of enclothment, according to Kabbalah, is God enclothing His infinite being in finite creation. This is alluded to in the numerical value of *Elokim*, "God," equaling the all-encompassing word for nature, *hateva*. In a sense, this is the paradigm for all further manifestations of enclothment.

Each morning as a man wraps his *tallit*, "prayer shawl," around him he recites the verses in Psalm 104 (1–2): "Bless God, O my soul. God, my God, You are very great. You have dressed Yourself in majesty and splendor, cloaked in light as with a garment, stretching out the heavens like a curtain." This is both beautiful poetry as well as being a description of the reality of God's enclothment in the world. (See Avraham Arieh Trugman, *The Mystical Nature of Light* [Jerusalem, NY: Simcha Press, 2007], p. 39.)

Man being created in God's image follows this same pattern of enclothment in the form of the soul descending from the upper spiritual worlds to dwell in the body. The soul, "an actual part of God Above," as taught in Chassidut, is enclothed in a body similar to how God is enclothed in the world. In an even deeper sense, Divinity is enclothed in the soul itself.

It further follows that all physical reality enclothes a deeper spiritual essence. One of the purposes of the mitzvot is to be continually involved in uplifting and transforming physical objects, deeds, and speech into spiritual essence. Each mitzvah is an opportunity to extract from physical reality its pure holy spark, revealing Divinity in the soul and in the world.

One of the deepest teachings of the Arizal describes a cataclysmic event in Creation's unfolding that he termed the "breaking of the vessels," when the initially immature vessels of Creation shattered from the influx of primordial light. He explains that this world, called *olam hatikkun*, the world of rectification, is comprised of the shattered vessels of a previous world. Each part of the shattered vessels enclothes a trapped spark of light, in need of repair and redemption. The paradigm of the present state of the world enclothing previous worlds in need of rectification is practically identical to the manner in which reincarnation is understood on an individual level.

In scientific terms this paradigm is revealed in the fabric of the universe, where matter enclothes energy. Below the surface of all matter is a hidden world of teeming energy and movement. Electromagnetism, the dynamic energy fueling the universe, consists of a subtle dance of attraction and repulsion, wave and particle, "run and return." Revelations in science over the course of the past century demonstrate an ongoing process of discovery, of finding more complex and smaller components of reality, each one successively containing even smaller particles and energy. String theory, the cutting edge of physics today, posits that the smallest particles of the universe are actually composed of infinitesimal vibrating strings whose "music" determines the physical parameters of all physical existence. Particles which appear as one dimensional points are, according to this theory, enclothing much more fundamental multidimensional strings.

Rabbi Yitzchak Ginsburgh teaches that the development of Kabbalah throughout the ages can be seen as revealed in three stages. Starting from the earliest transmission of the Jewish mystical tradition till the time of the Arizal, the teachings of Kabbalah could be defined as explaining creation's inner workings, the soul, the spiritual and physical worlds, and reality as a linear process of progressive unfolding called *hishtalshelut*. It was Rabbi Moshe Cordovero, who died right as the Arizal came to Safed, who first organized and systemized the Kabbalistic tradition up until his day in such a clear fashion.

The next stage of revelation, from the Arizal to the Ba'al Shem Tov, is called *hitlabeshut*, enclothment. The Arizal taught that many Kabbalistic concepts that had been revealed up to his time in a "one dimensional" form were in fact far more complex. His teachings of the soul, and the *sefirot* – the ten Divine emanations manifest in creation and the spiritual and physical worlds, exposed multifaceted dimensions till then hidden. Each entity in a complex structure was shown to be included in every other part of the system in a myriad of ways. He revealed layer upon layer of inner meaning in the written, oral, and mystical traditions and in the very fabric of reality. It is in this context that his teachings of reincarnation were revealed.

The final stage in the development of Kabbalah called *hashraʾah*, or direct experience of the Divine, was revealed by the Baʾal Shem Tov. Whereas the teachings of the Arizal in their textual form were incredibly intricate, and without proper explanation could only be understood by a relatively small and exclusive group, the teachings of the Baʾal Shem Tov sought to translate this profound wisdom in such a way that any person would be able to experience a direct and intimate relationship with God. That the teachings of the Arizal have had such a profound effect on Jewish thought is due in great part to the Baʾal Shem Tov translating them into a more simplified, accessible form.

In conclusion, we can state that to understand the Kabbalistic tradition of reincarnation entails seeing it operating in the overall context of cycles. A proper grasp of enclothment will further allow us to perceive how it actually works in all its myriad forms.

THE OBJECTIONS OF RABBI SAʾADYA GAON

When studying Talmud, one never discards a rejected view or an objection to a prevailing opinion. Instead, even though it has not been accepted, it is retained in the literature for a number of reasons, some of which are outlined in the first chapter of the Mishnah of *Eduyot*. Similarly, we need not discard the opinion of Rabbi Saʾadya Gaon simply because it was rejected by the Jewish mainstream. Actually, as we delve into his views as expressed in his book, *Emunot v'Deiʾot*, we will see that perhaps his opinion was not rejected after all!

As we study the work of Rabbi Saʾadya on our topic, we note that the term he uses for reincarnation is not gilgul, as we have earlier introduced, but *haʾataka*, which comes from the root meaning "to move" or "uproot." According to Rabbi Yitzchak Ginsburgh his choice of term sheds great light on his objection.

According to Rabbi Ginsburgh there is a subtle but very crucial difference between ha'ataka, which is best translated as "transmigration," and gilgul, "reincarnation." Transmigration means that a particular soul dies and then returns, intact, in a subsequent lifetime, in another body. This can happen many times, but each time it is the exact same soul which returns, just in different bodies. This is the standard way most people think of reincarnation, but this is not the tradition as taught by the Arizal (see Chapter Four). The Jewish view is far more complex and does not subscribe to the view that it is the very same soul returning in different lifetimes, as the word ha'ataka implies. Rather, gilgul is predicated on understanding that every soul contains many different levels, some active, and others relatively dormant. In addition, every soul is connected to higher and more inclusive soul roots. When a person dies, those parts of his or her soul that have been rectified are elevated and return to the soul root, never to return in a body, while those parts that are still in need of rectification return, but in a totally new constellation of soul forces. These "unrepaired" parts, aspects that either lay dormant or were tainted by sin, are joined by other sparks from the same soul root, other aspects also in need of rectification or levels of the person's soul that have not as yet descended into a body. The idea of active and dormant parts of the soul, according to Rabbi Ginsburgh, is reminiscent of recent revelations in genetics. Sometimes genes are active in a person's own lifetime, while at other times they are dormant and only become active when transmitted to the next generation.

Therefore, in the Kabbalistic tradition, it is never the exact same soul which returns; rather it is an entirely new incarnation, albeit with remnants of one soul's previous lifetimes impressed upon the new joining of soul to body. Whereas the emphasis of ha'ataka is on the soul which has, as it were, moved from one place or body to another, the stress of gilgul is on a body housing a new composite entity. The reason for this is that gilgul operates in the overall context of hitlabeshut, where a spiritual entity enclothes itself in a physical reality, which then becomes the arena for unification, elevation, and rectification.

We can now understand that Rabbi Sa'adya's objection to ha'ataka is actually shared by the Arizal, who focused on the tradition of gilgul as revealed in the *Bahir* and the *Zohar*. Whether Rabbi Sa'adya would have approved of gilgul had he known of the authentic Kabbalistic tradition we can only guess, but it is reasonable to think that he would have had nothing against the true Kabbalistic tradition.

PURPOSE, RECTIFICATION, AND JUDGMENT

Returning to the idea of how concepts need to be understood in context leads us to examine some of reincarnation's basic premises and their correlation to fundamental principles of Judaism.

Reincarnation is based on the basic Jewish belief that creation has an overall purpose and is divinely guided towards the ultimate fulfillment of that purpose. Each individual soul, created in the "image of God," has a mission, and that is to come and realize its own lofty stature. If it is unable to accomplish this mission in one lifetime it is given further opportunities, as "neither does God take away life but devises means that none is lost to Him" (2 Samuel 14:14). It was God's will that the soul descend from its pure spiritual state in order to achieve through its sojourn in the physical world, also known as *olam hatikkun*, "world of rectification," an even higher level than it would have been able to attain by remaining in the upper spiritual worlds. Reincarnation, or gilgul, allows the mission to be accomplished over the course of more than just one lifetime.

In a number of places in the Talmud it is stated that by performing certain mitzvot a Jew becomes a partner with God in the purpose of creation. The Arizal expanded upon this idea and taught that it was the mission of the Jewish people to find all the hidden sparks of light and holiness trapped in the broken vessels constituting this world and to uplift and redeem them. When enough segments of reality are repaired, it will create the proper momentum and produce the ideal conditions for the inauguration of the Messianic era.

One of the beliefs strongly held in the Jewish tradition insists on there being a reason for everything and a purpose for all of God's creations. This is coupled with a second belief affirming all of God's actions to be for the ultimate benefit of His creations. Clearly we are not always able to fathom those reasons, but once we realize that not everything that happens to us results from an accounting in just this life, it opens up a whole new vista on viewing reality in a larger context.

Along with the belief in a Divine plan for creation and the central role of rectification in that plan, intrinsic to the understanding of gilgul is the overall concept of judgment, that every soul is judged and must make an accounting of all its deeds after it departs the body, the results of which determine its future. "There is a judge and there is judgment" (*Leviticus Rabba* 30).

Judgment does not take place only once at the end of one's life. We are taught that man is being judged throughout his lifetime. Rosh Hashana, the Jewish New Year, is not a wild day of abandon; it is a time for deep introspection and a day for God's judgment. Rosh Hashana is preceded by the month of Elul, more time for an individual to take a personal accounting of his or her actions over the course of the previous year, and itself begins the Days of Awe, ten days of further reflection on life and our place in it, which culminate with Yom Kippur. And despite the seriousness with which one must approach this time of year, it is not a period of sadness or despair. On the contrary – the gifts of repentance, atonement, and forgiveness allow us to feel a sense of great inner joy.

Judgment is not to be perceived in negative terms, nor should it be viewed as vindictive; it is part and parcel of the very fabric of the spiritual and the physical worlds. The name Elokim, which as we pointed out has the same numerical value as hateva, "nature," is that name of God associated with judgment, law, and strength. This aspect is manifest in the consistent and dependable laws of nature that rule every aspect of physical reality. Just as the universe operates according to set laws, so too do set laws regulate the spiritual worlds. In fact, these two sets of laws are mirror images of each other.

In truth, it is God's great kindness, represented by His four letter name, which is the ultimate force behind nature's laws and the aspect of judgment. According to Chassidut, the verse in Psalms (84:12) that demonstrates the relationship between these two names of God and what they represent is, "The sun and its shield [is comparable to] *Hashem* [God's four letter name] Elokim." God in His aspect of mercy is like the sun, the source of light, while Elokim is the shield, the actual manifestation of light in this world.

These two names of God and the seemingly opposite aspects of mercy and judgment they represent are unified in the Shema, the cardinal statement of faith in the Torah: "Hear (i.e., understand), O Israel, Hashem is our God [Elokim], Hashem is one" (Deuteronomy 6:4). At the very end of *Neila*, the final and climactic prayer of Yom Kippur, the congregation declares seven times: "Hashem, He is Elokim." In this way we conclude the forty day period from the beginning of Elul till the end of the ten Days of Awe with a full appreciation that judgment is ultimately motivated by God's great love and mercy.

This same idea is also revealed in the numeric value of gilgul, seventy-two, being the same as *chessed*, mercy and loving-kindness (analyzing the numeric value of a Hebrew word is part of a method of study called *gematria*, which will be discussed later). Although it may appear that reincarnation is a judgment and punishment for the soul's sins, mistakes, and omissions, in truth, it is God's merciful gift of an opportunity for repair and healing. *This idea is crucial for a true appreciation of the role reincarnation plays in God's overall purpose and plan for humanity.*

In a number of places in *Netivot Shalom*, the Slonimer Rebbe's classic commentary on the five books of Moses and other assorted subjects, he states that every person comes into the world with a particular purpose and specific repairs to accomplish, and how it is of crucial importance for an individual to fulfill his or her mission in this world. He then asks: How can a person truly know what that purpose and rectification is? He answers that one way for us to know is by paying attention to those things we find particularly difficult and challenging to do – those are the very things we need to fix, and that is why they are so hard for us. In the act of rectification, we come to fulfill our purpose in the world.

After Jacob fought with the angel he was given the new name "Israel." The Torah defines this name: "for you strove with God and man and prevailed" (Genesis 32:29). Meeting the challenges of life is not necessarily easy or painless, yet when we rise to the occasion we are fulfilling the reason for our existence. The word for "test" and the word meaning to "lift up" share the same root, teaching us that every test and challenge in life is meant ultimately to raise us up to new heights we could not have achieved otherwise.

When investigating the concept of judgment from a Jewish perspective two ideas come to the fore. First is the correlation of cause, effect, and consequences in relation to judgment and punishment. Second is the ever-present theme in any treatment of the subject, the dynamic called "a measure for a measure." These two ideas are intrinsically woven together in any Jewish notion of judgment.

Many times what is felt and experienced as judgment and punishment is in truth simply the consequences of our actions. Every thought, speech, and action produces a result, a subtle ripple effect of consequences. For most people these connections are hidden and may even seem non-consequential, but Jewish belief is premised on the idea that everything matters, everything is recorded, and all must be accounted for. This sentiment is expressed succinctly by Rabbi Akiba in parable form in *Pirkei Avot* (3:20):

> "Everything is given on collateral and a net is spread over all the living. The shop is open; the Merchant extends credit; the ledger is open; the hand writes; and whoever wishes to borrow, let him come and borrow. The collectors make their rounds constantly, every day, and collect payment from the person, whether he realizes it or not. They have proof to rely upon; and the judgment is a truthful judgment; and everything is prepared for the [final festive] banquet."

This profound parable encapsulates countless statements from throughout Jewish tradition relating to the nature of judgment, the belief in the righteousness of God's ways, and the parameters within which man operates in this world. It is in this context too that reincarnation functions.

"A measure for a measure," a phrase very similar to the notion of cause and effect, could be described as the working mechanism of judgment, the particular way effects follow from causes. It is the manner in which the consequences of our actions play themselves out. Similar to the physical law that every action has an equal and opposite reaction, "a measure for a measure" is its spiritual counterpart. Sometimes the reaction is immediate, and in those cases we have the best chance of recognizing intuitively this dynamic at work. Other times the consequences are meted out over days, weeks, months, or years. The older one gets and the more mature spiritually he or she becomes, the easier it becomes to see the incredible web of Divine judgment. Reincarnation just extends the playing field by recognizing that sometimes it even takes many lifetimes till the score is finally settled. It takes a very broad level of consciousness to be aware of the wider context of the soul's journey and its ultimate purpose.

REINCARNATION IN LIGHT OF THE HEBREW LETTERS

[The section discussing the letters of the Hebrew word for "reincarnation" is based on the teachings of Rabbi Yitzchak Ginsburgh in his book *The Hebrew Letters* (Jerusalem: Gal Einai Publications, 1990), a work I was privileged to assist in writing. The parts relating to the word *gal* are based on an appendix found at the end of Rabbi Ginsburgh's book *Muda'ut Tiv'it* (Rechovot: Gal Einai Publications, 1999).]

In Hebrew, the name of an entity is more than a linguistic symbol by which it is designated, rather it is considered its very essence and life force, bringing it into being and animating its continued existence. The Hebrew letters are channels of infinite Divine creative consciousness pervading all levels of reality. Similar to how a scientist looks at atoms, particles, molecules, and elements as the building blocks of creation, the student of Torah, and particularly Kabbalah, views the Hebrew alphabet in the same way. To truly understand any word or concept in Torah we must first look at the meaning of the individual letters literally spelling out the concept, and then analyze the entire word and its many rich levels of association. In this light, we will now try to understand the deeper meanings of reincarnation, gilgul, according to the Hebrew letters.

The letters comprising the word gilgul, גלגול, are *gimmel*, *lamed*, and *vav*. As mentioned before, gal, גל, is repeated twice to emphasize its cyclic nature, or as in the vision of Ezekiel, a wheel within a wheel.

The Gimmel

ג

The form of the letter gimmel is reminiscent of a foot slightly bent forward, indicating a person in motion. The gimmel represents the constant dynamic of "run and return" as it manifests itself in all cycles of nature, as well as in human physiology, as discussed above. Gilgul is the manifestation of the run and return of the soul between life and death, between this world and the upper spiritual worlds.

The name of the letter gimmel is paradoxical in that as a verb (*gamal, ligmol*) it means both "to give" and "to wean." The paradox is further strengthened because the giving can be as reward or as punishment. Weaning or withholding can also be viewed as a positive giving in that it facilitates independence and self-identity. As we have seen, the purpose of Divine reward and punishment, as well as mercy and judgment, are ultimately the same – man's rectification in the fullest sense by realizing his or her full potential as an image of God.

As a noun (*gamal*), the gimmel means "camel," a symbol of both life and death. The camel wandering through the desert represents man's journey through life, the stage upon which he runs and returns in constant striving. In ancient times the camel was seen as a benevolent symbol in that nothing could accompany man through the desert as well as a camel who held within himself enough water to survive the harsh desert conditions. On the other hand, the camel sometimes symbolizes the angel of death who thrives in the lifeless wastelands of the desert (*Zohar* 2:236a).

In Aramaic, a language used in many holy texts and which is very similar to Hebrew, the root of gimmel means "bridge." Gilgul is thus the bridge between life and death. As we will see, it is not only a result of the further need for repair of the soul, and thus an extension of the concept of punishment, but it can also be viewed as bestowing an individual with another lifetime in which to make further spiritual advances, and thus it can be seen as an extension of the concept of reward.

One further reflection regarding reward and punishment is that they both imply free will, for without the freedom to choose, reward and punishment would have no real meaning. The act of running represented by the gimmel expresses the power of will and free choice, as the root for the word "run," *ratz*, can be related to that of "will," *ratzon*. The motion of running is also similar to the dynamic of run and return, as the feet alternate being in contact with the earth and lifted in mid-air.

Free will is one of the principle beliefs in Judaism. Maimonides, in particular, was a strong proponent of the importance of the concept. Another fundamental principle of Jewish faith is that of Divine Providence and Omnipotence. How both Divine Providence and free will can exist side by side is a paradox, and yet the Torah embraces both concepts, despite their appearing to be mutually exclusive. The gimmel, meaning reward and punishment, which is predicated on Divine involvement in human affairs, also implies free will, alluding to this enigmatic paradox.

There is a major disagreement between Maimonides and Nachmanides regarding the nature of the World to Come, the time of ultimate reward. Maimonides believed that the World to Come would be a purely spiritual world, a world of souls without bodies. Nachmanides argued that since the deeds of man were performed, and his free will was expressed, in the physical world, when the soul inhabits a body, then the reward earned by those deeds will be presented in the physical plane, too. Kabbalah and Chassidut agree with the opinion as stated by Nachmanides.

The position of Nachmanides is very much in line with the concept of reincarnation. Just as the soul returns to a body in order to accomplish its rectification and fulfill its ultimate purpose instead of receiving its reward or punishment after death in the spiritual world of souls alone, so too at the time of the final reward the soul will receive its reward in the resurrected body. The unity of spiritual and physical, a major goal of all the mitzvot, and Jewish life and thought in general, becomes the context of the ultimate reward of all the cycles of reincarnation a person goes through.

The Lamed
ל

The lamed is the tallest of the letters and represents the aspiration of the heart. In Hebrew the word for "heart," *lev*, begins with a lamed. The root of the name of the letter lamed means both "learn" and "teach," and its numerical value is thirty. Reincarnation in its very essence exists in order that the soul will learn and then apply that learning in order to advance spiritually. Reincarnation is closely connected to the concept of teshuva, "repentance," or literally "returning" to God and one's true soul essence. Maimonides, when discussing the laws regarding teshuva, states that a person can consider his or her teshuva complete when they are put back into the same situation in which they had initially sinned but this time demonstrate a proper response (*Mishneh Torah, Hilchot Teshuva* 2:1). This is the exact purpose of gilgul.

The aspiring heart represented by the lamed desires not only to learn the lessons of life and teach them to others but longs to elevate itself in order to be close to God. This is represented in the lamed stretching itself above all the other letters. While the gimmel symbolizes touching the earth with its foot, the lamed is propelled upward towards the heavens. These two opposite but complementary motions once again relate to the dynamic of run and return, as well as the unity of body and soul, physical and spiritual.

The number thirty, the numeric value of the lamed, relates to the monthly cycle of the moon, which is especially important in Torah, as the Jewish calendar is based on the lunar cycle (with due consideration of the solar cycle as well). The waxing and the waning of the moon are intrinsically tied to the cycles of reincarnation and all other cycles as well. Although the word galgal describes the orbit of all the planets, the "orbit of the moon," *galgal hayareach*, is most associated with that term.

The Vav

ו

The last of the letters comprising the word gilgul is a vav, whose shape is similar to a pillar or a man standing upright with his feet on the earth and his head reaching to the heavens. This is the same image as represented by the combination of the gimmel and the lamed, as mentioned above.

Vav means "hook," a connector, and when used at the beginning of a word means "and," the grammatical manner of connecting two ideas in a sentence. A unique and profound quality of the vav in biblical Hebrew is that when appearing at the beginning of a verb it changes the tense of the verb to its opposite – past to future and future to past. In relation to gilgul the vav is the connector between lifetimes, the power to manifest the past in the present and through teshuva to draw upon the future to rectify the past. This idea can be seen in the enigmatic statement in the Talmud that when one does teshuva from fear, he is able to change past deliberate transgressions into inadvertent ones, whereas doing teshuva from love, transforms past sins into merits (*Yoma* 86b). This of course can occur in one lifetime, but it also applies to doing teshuva in a future incarnation for mistakes made in previous ones.

In the Tabernacle in the desert, the curtains were connected to the pillars by way of hooks. Interestingly, both the form of the letter vav – shaped like a pillar and its meaning of "hook" – appear together in the phrase "the hooks of the pillars" (Exodus 27:10). Curtains hide what is behind them and therefore represent concealment, while pillars stand tall and dignified, symbolizing revelation. It is the function of the vav, the "hook," to unite these two opposites. This reminds us of the concept of enclothment, having a relatively higher level hidden in a relatively lower level, where concealment is only temporary, and whose real function is to reveal. Gilgul also conceals past lifetimes in the present for the purpose of revealing an even greater level of repair.

Before we delve into the meaning of gal, it is worthwhile to look at one more Hebrew letter having a deep connection to reincarnation. The letter *tav*, ת, is shaped like a stamp or seal, which is appropriate for it is the last of the twenty-two Hebrew letters. Its name means a "sign," "mark," or "impression," which is likewise connected to its shape. In one of Ezekiel's prophesies, a man goes through the city of Jerusalem setting a mark, a "tav," upon the foreheads of all those to be saved (Ezekiel 9:4–6). It is also the secret of why the Torah's account of Creation ends with a tav, "that God created to do [la'asot]" (Genesis 2:3). It is also the secret of why the word for "death," *mavet*, ends with a tav.

Impressions of previous states of being are seen at every level of reality; from fossils to geographical landscapes, from an inherited genetic code to psychological states of mind, from footprints in the sand to a butterfly emerging from its chrysalis, which it had entered as a caterpillar. In relation to souls, reincarnation is the impression of previous lifetimes stamped upon a person's present reality. The tav more than any other letter represents the statement in *Sefer Yetzirah* (10:7): "The end is imbedded in the beginning and the beginning in the end." For the soul this is manifest in reincarnation, when death is connected to a new beginning, a renewed life for the soul in a new body. The Jewish songwriter and performer Bob Dylan expressed the intrinsic connection between life and death this way: "He not busy being born is busy dying."

The component letters comprising the tav (which in the Torah looks like this: ת), are a *dalet*, ד, and a *nun*, נ, spelling *dan*, to judge. The seal of life is death and the stamp in which the end connects to the beginning is through judgment. Significantly, the only name of God used in the initial account of Creation is Elokim, the name of God associated with judgment. In the second account of Creation, which fills in additional details and gives added perspective, the four-letter name of God first appears, teaching us once again the inherent connection of God's attributes of mercy and judgment.

It is significant that the term for the resurrection of the dead, *techiyat hameitim*, begins with a tav, for "the end is imbedded in the beginning and the beginning in the end."

There are three essential services of the soul, all of which begin with the letter tav: teshuva – "repentance," *tefilla* – "prayer," and the study and fulfillment of *Torah*. These three services of the soul correspond to the three patriarchs: Abraham is associated with *teshuva*, as he was the first to return to the true knowledge of God; Isaac relates to *tefilla*, as he led a life of prayer and contemplative meditation; and Jacob corresponds to *Torah*, for he spent most of his life in the tents of Torah.

The three patriarchs along with King David form the "four feet of the chariot," the four foundations on which all the worlds rest (*Zohar* 1:248b). David represents *tikkun*, "rectification," also beginning with the letter tav. All four of these services of the soul relate directly to reincarnation. We have already discussed the connection of teshuva and tikkun to gilgul, and in subsequent chapters we will discuss the intrinsic connection of Torah and tefilla.

The tav also relates to *malchut*, kingship, the last of the ten sefirot (malchut also concludes with a tav). "Your kingdom is the kingdom of all the worlds" represents the enclothment of God in all the spiritual and physical worlds (Psalms 145:13). Each Divine enclothment leaves its impression on that world, ultimately linking all worlds together. This impression impacts upon the soul and is manifested in the soul's longing to transcend the limited ego and to unite with God. It also motivates a desire to transcend the limits of the particulars of this lifetime in order to see beyond to the root of the soul and its true history. One does not have to actually know the details of previous lifetimes in order to sense the *tikkunim* (pl. for *tikkun*, "rectifications") needed in the present moment. It is enough to direct the soul towards the four areas of service mentioned above to draw a future vision of perfection that will transform and rectify the past, while yet in the present.

We will now delve into the varied meanings and associations of gal in order to apprehend a deeper and richer appreciation of the overriding context of reincarnation. Many of the meanings of gal relate to cycles, circles, and wheels. Gilgul in its simple understanding is based on the repeating cycle of life, death, and life, the circle dance of the soul from one life to another, as alluded to in the vision of the chariot: a wheel within a wheel.

Numerous words that have an association with circles are

based on gal. A mound of stones is referred to as *gal avanim*, rolling the Torah closed after it has been read is called *gelila*, and a wave of water is a *gal mayim*. As a verb *gal* means to roll, revolve, turn around, and reincarnate. A very famous figure in the Talmud was called *Choni Hame'agel*, Choni, the Circle Maker.

A fascinating phenomenon found in many Hebrew roots is that words connoting opposite meanings have the very same root letters. This idea is symbolically expressed by *agol*, something round and circular, and by galgal, "wheel" or "cycle," objects which tend to be inclusive, bringing together all the points on the circle equally. It further shows a deep intrinsic connection between two seemingly opposite concepts.

One of the most important cycles to manifest itself on multiple levels of reality is the cycle of exile and redemption. The winter months, in which nature goes dormant, trees shed their leaves, and there is a feeling of cold, bareness, and lifelessness, are comparable to exile. The spring months, with their bursting energy of life renewed and warmth, are associated with redemption.

The cycle of exile and redemption and slavery and freedom, forms the backdrop for all Jewish history. We were born as a nation through the experience of slavery and the subsequent redemption from Egypt. The cycle of exile, slavery, and persecution, followed by freedom and redemption was repeated throughout the period of the Judges and Prophets, and especially in the four major exiles of Babylonia, Persia, Greece, and Rome. In addition, for two thousand years smaller communities scattered throughout the Diaspora experienced expulsions, crusades, inquisitions, pogroms, and holocaust. Yet each time the Jewish people managed to avert total disaster and renew itself.

The very first narrative of exile in the Bible is the story of Adam and Eve's expulsion from the utopian state of the Garden of Eden. This archetypal story becomes the paradigm for the basic existential condition of man in the world. On an individual level each person experiences exile in the emotional and psychological forms of sadness, depression, low self-esteem, and loneliness, while redemption is experienced in love, accomplishment, self-expression, and joy.

Therefore, it is deeply revealing that these two opposite states – "exile," *gola* or *galut,* and "redemption," *geula* – both share the letters of gal. This teaches us that in essence exile and redemption are part of a bigger framework and are intrinsically linked to each other. We can see this in nature, history, and daily experience. Light is all the brighter when it follows darkness, and revelation is greater when it is preceded by concealment. The word for revelation also contains the same letters as gal, as does one of the words for joy, *gila.* Revealing what was previously hidden in most cases leads to great inner joy and a feeling of personal redemption, especially when the revelation is of a spiritual nature. Yet sometimes what has been hidden and subsequently revealed leads to just the opposite – to disgust, *ga'al* and loneliness, *galmud.* Once again we see opposites united by mutual letters, informing us to look deeper to see how they are inherently interwoven.

Of course, all these insights related to gal impact on our understanding of reincarnation. Even deeper than the associated meanings of cycles and circles, gilgul is essentially bound to the specific cycle of exile and redemption. Yet we can see it from two distinct perspectives. On the one hand, life can be a state of redemption, while death represents the epitome of exile. On the other hand, from the point of view of a pure soul coming from the upper worlds down to this earth, life here can be seen as a state of exile, while death brings with it redemption and the return of the soul to its heavenly abode. There is truth in both these perspectives and only by unifying them do we arrive at a true understanding of the soul and its ultimate purpose.

Earlier we learned that good things come about through the agency of good people, while bad things come about through the agency of bad people. The verb used for "come about" is related to gal. The way life unfolds is reminiscent of ocean waves, *galei mayim,* each individual wave follows another, each one invisibly linked and dependent on all the other waves. Every cause has an effect, and every effect has a cause. A measure has a countermeasure and nothing escapes notice or passes without impacting on something else. Leaves of autumn fall to the ground where they turn into mulch and nourish new life. Life leads to death and death to life in an ongoing cycle of existence. Even the definition of death and life become somewhat elusive, as expressed in the Talmudic statement that the righteous are called alive even after death, while evil ones are called dead even when alive (*Berachot* 18a–b).

When one unrolls a scroll, he reveals what is inside and when one rolls it up, he conceals what lies within. Gilgul operates in a similar manner, hiding previous causes and effects in a new composite of body and soul, while simultaneously revealing through the circumstances of life opportunities for healing and fixing both the present and the past.

One of the greatest joys possible lies in feeling that life is full of purpose and significance. This is achieved by revealing one's inner potential, consisting of layer upon layer of previous circumstance and inherited possibility. The deeper we delve into the depths of the soul the more is revealed about what we need to do in the here and now to maximize that hidden potential.

Another word relating to gal is *gulgolet*, "skull," due to its round shape. In Kabbalah, *gulgalta*, an exalted level of Divine consciousness, is associated with *keter*, "crown," the highest of all sefirot. It is here in the furthest reaches of the higher worlds that gilgul and all the associated meanings discussed above have their spiritual source. According to Kabbalah it is at this level that God first enclothes Himself in lower levels of creation. God as First Cause sets in motion all existence, the impression and ripples that are experienced at all levels of reality. A dramatic example is the ongoing effects on creation of the Big Bang; a more subtle image is of a pebble tossed upon a smooth lake and the circular ripples that ensue. In man these ripples are embedded in the deepest recesses of the psyche, affected by both Divinity's impression on all physical and spiritual existence, as well as the entire history of each individual soul and its complex connection to every other soul going back to the very first human beings. Probing these profound secrets of life is where true revelation is found.

CHAPTER THREE:

Implications of Reincarnation

$\mathfrak{A}$lthough we touched on a number of important corollaries which go hand in hand with a belief in reincarnation in the last chapter, we did not elaborate all of them. In this chapter we will discuss additional significant assumptions and implications.

It may go without saying that an acceptance of the reality of gilgul assumes a belief in a soul and an afterlife, but since there is much confusion among people regarding these concepts, it is well worth our while to investigate both the Jewish view of the soul and the belief in an afterlife.

We begin with the primary source of the Bible to see evidence of the existence of the soul: "And Hashem Elokim formed man of the dust of the earth and breathed into his nostrils the soul of life and man became a living being" (Genesis 2:7). The term for "living being," *nefesh chaya*, is used for other animals as well, but the term "the soul of life," *nishmat chaim*, is one used exclusively for man. Rashi on this verse explains that the "dust of the earth" represents the physical component of man, his more animal nature, while the "soul of life" symbolizes the spiritual element, an ingredient exclusive to man. In addition, only man is described as being created "in the image of God" (Genesis 1:26–27).

Nachmanides explains that the image depicted here of God

blowing into the nostrils of man the "soul of life" teaches us that God is imparting to the human something of His essence, for one who blows, does so from his very innards. In this sense the creation of the soul differs from all other creations as it emanates, as it were, from the very inner essence of God. The Ba'al Shem Tov paraphrased a verse in Job (31:12) to explain that the soul is "an actual part of God Above." To this the Alter Rebbe, Rabbi Shneur Zalman of Liady, added an exclamation at the end: *mamash*! A very hard word to translate exactly, mamash means "for real!" Another important verse in this same spirit from Proverbs (20:27) states: "The candle of God is the soul of man."

Among the many explanations of what it means to be created in the image of God is included the idea that the soul inside the human is of an eternal nature and also that it has free choice, both being crucial elements in any understanding of a Jewish view of the afterlife. Indeed, the entire oral tradition is based on the assumption that a person is judged after his or her death and that there is an afterlife. This is why there are countless statements and descriptions of these matters in the Talmud, Midrash, and Kabbalah, as well as laws and customs based on these beliefs. Intrinsic to these traditions is the belief in the World to Come, a time in the future when the final reward will be given to each person for their actions in this world.

Despite the fact that it would be impossible to bring the many references to the soul, its nature, and the belief in an afterlife, in a relatively short book such as ours, it is still important to quote a few of those texts to give the reader a notion of how Jewish tradition relates to these matters.

Upon waking in the morning the first thing a Jew exclaims is: "I gratefully thank You, O living and eternal King, for You have returned my soul within me with compassion; abundant is Your faithfulness." Sleep is considered one-sixtieth of death (*Berachot* 57a), therefore we thank God for returning our soul to our body and giving us another day of life, something we should never take for granted. We can relate this idea in the bigger picture to reincarnation as well. Gilgul has the same numeric value as chessed, "loving-kindness," and should be seen as God's compassion and abundant faithfulness in giving us another opportunity of life.

Another very important statement recited first thing in the morning emphasizes the soul and its relationship to God: "My God, the soul You placed within me is pure. You created it, You fashioned it, You breathed it into me. You safeguard it within me and eventually You will take it from me and restore it to me in the Time to Come. As long as the soul is within me I gratefully thank You, Hashem, my God, and God of my forefathers, Master of all works, God of all souls. Blessed are You, God, who restores souls to dead bodies." Although the "dead bodies" referred to here are the bodies that rise from their nightly slumber, it is also an allusion to the final resurrection of the dead, which will take place in the future, preceding the World to Come. In addition, it describes the same dynamic as the cycle of reincarnation.

In *Pirkei Avot*, one of the most important compilations of basic Jewish beliefs and world view, there are numerous references to the purpose of the soul, free choice, and judgment, and the belief in an afterlife. Among them are the following, which emphasize the intrinsic connection between our deeds in this world and what we can expect in the future:

> "Rabbi Jacob said: This world is like a lobby before the World to Come; prepare yourself in the lobby so that you may enter the banquet hall" (4:21).
> "He used to say: Better one hour of repentance and good deeds in this world than the entire life of the World to Come; and better one hour of spiritual bliss in the World to Come than the entire life of this world" (4:22).

One of the most comprehensive statements that include so much of Jewish belief was transmitted by Rabbi Elazar Hakappar:

"He used to say: The newborn will die; the dead will live again; the living will be judged – in order that they come to know, make aware [to others], and become aware that He is God, He is the Fashioner, He is the Creator, He is the Discerner, He is the Judge, He is the Witness, He is the Plaintiff, He will Judge. Blessed is He, Who does not act iniquitously, nor does He forget, or [show] favoritism, or accept a bribe, for everything is His. Know that everything is according to the reckoning. And let not your evil inclination promise you that the grave will be an escape for you – for against your will you are created; against your will you are born; against your will you live; against your will you die, and against your will you are destined to give an account before the King Who rules over kings, the Holy One, Blessed is He" (4:29).

Although there are a few statements in Jewish texts that could be read as if only darkness and silence follows death, these need to be put in perspective with the overwhelming number of references to the eternity of the soul. The proper manner to understand these verses is that they express and emphasize that even though the soul returns to God, the body returns to the earth and there, it, not the soul, meets darkness and silence. Only as long as the soul is in the body can they mutually enjoy the gift of life in this world, therefore we are warned to take advantage of it while the gift is available.

An important related point is that although we are promised reward in the World to Come for what we accomplish here, we are advised to put that promise to the side and to serve God in this world for no ulterior motive:

"Antigonus, leader of Socho, received the tradition from Simon the Righteous. He used to say: Be not like servants who serve their master for the sake of receiving a reward; instead be like servants who serve their master not for the sake of receiving a reward. And let the awe of Heaven be upon you" (1:3).

Despite the great emphasis on the World to Come and promises of future reward, the fact that Judaism has remained very oriented to living in this world is to the credit of the Jewish people. The exclamation of *Lechaim!* ("to life!"), used so prevalently in Jewish life, speaks volumes of the love of life and the determination to live fully in the here and now, yet without falling into the trap of hedonism and "live today for tomorrow we will die." In truth this is not an easy tightrope to walk, but one the sages have encouraged us to do. It is reported of Rabbi Shneur Zalman of Liady that he once exclaimed to God: "I don't want Your reward and I don't want Your World to Come – I want You!"

Jewish belief in the soul and the afterlife is not only confined to the realm of philosophy but is established in custom and law, especially in relationship to death and mourning. Although it may appear that the laws regarding mourning exist to assist the mourner deal with his or her grief, this in truth is only half the story. Jewish texts reveal that the soul departing the body is equally in need of comfort and assistance and is very much aware of what is happening below, especially to its previous body.

The many laws regarding the treatment of a body from the time of death through its interment are designed not only to give the physical body that housed a holy soul honor – a body after death is compared to a Torah scroll which must be respectfully buried if it has become unfit for further use – but it is also considered a source of great comfort to the now dispossessed soul.

The respect afforded the body after death is in keeping with the basic Jewish belief of seeing the physical as intrinsically bound to the spiritual. That is why teachings regarding the resurrection of the dead all emphasize that true rectification must take place in the context of the unity of soul and body, spiritual and physical. It is this same teaching that lies at the heart of gilgul. The soul, after living in this world, cannot fully atone for or repair itself in the upper worlds alone; it must return to the very context of this world in order to complete its purpose and tikkun.

The different stages of the mourning process, the seven days, one month, and one year periods, are not only psychologically sound and sensitive to the needs of the mourners, but correspond to the different periods of judgment, cleansing, and clarification the soul experiences as it ascends from level to level in the upper worlds. In fact we are taught that the laws of mourning, especially the daily recitation of *kaddish*, the mourner's prayer, assist the departed soul as much as the ones left behind. The entire Jewish mourning process can be seen as a sensitively crafted parallel progression leading to both the comfort of the mourner and the elevation of the departed soul.

An excellent book that discusses the belief in the soul and the afterlife in light of modern scientific inquiry is *Soul Searching: Seeking Scientific Ground for the Jewish Tradition of an Afterlife* by Rabbi Yaacov Astor (Israel: Targum/Feldheim, 2003). This short but very thorough treatment of the subject, including reincarnation, from both a Jewish perspective and in light of impressive scientific research is highly recommended. Rabbi Astor cites Jewish traditions associated with the afterlife and compares them to the growing body of research by doctors, psychologists, and scientists into near death experiences and hypnotic states that reveal past lifetimes. While a Torah belief in the existence of the soul, its eternal nature, and reincarnation is not based nor dependent on science, yet it is certainly fascinating when scientific research based on thousands of independent experiences confirms many of the basic beliefs of Judaism.

WHY BAD THINGS HAPPEN TO GOOD PEOPLE

As we have already noted, the basic premise of reincarnation is intrinsically bound to the idea of Divine judgment. Therefore it behooves us to delve deeper into the nature of judgment and its impact on the process of gilgul.

One of the most frequently asked questions concerning God's stewardship of the world seeks to understand why it oftentimes appears that the righteous suffer and the evil prosper. This question symbolizes the overall attempt to understand how evil, suffering, and randomness all seem to exist in a world created by an all-powerful, omniscient, and merciful God. Even someone as great and wise as Moses failed to fully grasp the answer to this perplexing dilemma, as he is understood to have asked this very same question in a dialogue between him and God recorded in Exodus (33:13) and as explained by the Talmud (*Berachot* 7a). Although many possibilities are proposed by the sages, no clear, definitive answer is reached. The verse in Exodus (33:19): "And I will be gracious to whom I will be gracious and will show mercy on whom I will show mercy," which is quoted in the Talmudic discussion, leaves us feeling that the true answer is beyond man's capability of understanding.

The sentiment that God's logic and reasoning lie above human comprehension is best described by Isaiah (55:8–9): "'For My thoughts are not your thoughts, neither are your ways My ways,' says God. 'For as the heavens are higher than the earth, so are My ways higher than your ways and My thoughts higher than your thoughts.'" Similarly in *Pirkei Avot* (4:19) it is stated: "Rabbi Jannai said: It is not in our power to explain either the tranquility of the wicked or the suffering of the righteous." Rebbe Nachman of Breslov explained that it is actually quite natural that we do not understand all of God's ways. For if we did, in a sense, we would be limiting our concept of God to conform to our limited intelligence, when in truth, God is far greater and exalted above any true comprehension (*Likutei Moharan* 2:62).

In essence this was the predicament of Job as he struggled to understand his own suffering. The entire book of Job, considered the most philosophical of all the books of the Bible, is dedicated to these difficult questions of suffering and understanding God's ways. It is interesting to note that according to most opinions the book of Job was written by Moses, who also pondered these deep questions (*Baba Batra* 14b).

The book of Job ends with no real resolution, but God responds to Job with a list of fifty searing questions into the nature and secrets of creation. Job is unable to respond and in a state of awe comes to realize the limits of his ability to understand God's concealed ways. The realization of there being a hidden answer to the mysterious manner in which God directs the world was in the end a comfort to him.

We are not privy to the exact manner in which God decides upon and dispenses judgment; nonetheless, we are taught many general principles based upon which we can try to make sense out of suffering and other apparent "verdicts" that at first glance strain a reasonable understanding of the world around us and our own lives.

The first and perhaps foremost teaching regarding these matters is the firm belief that despite appearances God's judgments are righteous and true: "The Creator whose actions are perfect, for all His ways are just. He is a truthful God, never acting iniquitously; righteous and honest is He" (Deuteronomy 32:4). This core belief accompanies a Jew throughout life and it is one of the most fundamental doctrines on which a life of faith is based. Even at a funeral when the deceased lies before the mourners, they recite verses signaling their acceptance of God's judgment, for God gives and God takes away. Parallel teachings in the Talmud to this effect include, "All that God does, He does for the good" (*Berachot* 60b), "This [a seemingly negative occurrence] is also for the good" (*Ta'anit* 21a), and "A person is obligated to bless on negative tidings in the same manner as he blesses on the good" (*Mishnah, Berachot* 9:5).

Although "man was born to toil," this is not a curse, rather our fate and destiny (Job 5:7). God's greatest goodness is in granting us free will and the opportunity to earn eternal reward in the World to Come, and further, to actualize our potential to be a true image of God. That this comes through hard work, commitment, and at times suffering is, as it were, the rules of the game, the parameters in which the individual lives and ultimately dies.

56

The sages explain in many different places and in various ways that suffering, although not a necessarily preferred state of being, has many positive aspects. Suffering is considered atonement for misdeeds and a merciful way for God to exact judgment in this world, so that He can then pay a full reward to the person in the World to Come. Rashi, on the end of the passage – "Know that *Hashem* your God is *the* Judge, a faithful God, who reserves the covenant and loving-kindness for those that love Him and keep His commandments for a thousand generations, *and recompenses those that hate Him to their face in order to destroy them...*," comments that God pays evil ones any good they may do to their face, meaning, in this world in order to destroy them in the World to Come (Deuteronomy 7:10). The inverse is assumed as well – God pays the righteous in this world for any shortcomings in order to pay them for a thousand generations in the World to Come. This verse is one of the main sources for understanding the way in which God puts His judgments into effect. Similarly we are taught that the righteous are judged to a hairsbreadth in order to clean their slate in this world so that they will be free to rise to great heights in the next world.

Suffering is meant to cause us to reflect upon our deeds and direction in life and commit to repairing our actions. It is one of the greatest impetuses for doing teshuva, and in this sense is a means to refine and purify the soul. It is like one who becomes ill and sees in his or her sickness a wake-up call to adopt a healthier lifestyle. If one learns the proper lesson from the sickness, in retrospect it will be seen as a hidden blessing. Suffering and illness are also reminders for us to not take good health for granted. We should realize that not to be burdened with physical pain and discomfort is in itself a blessing, and not just the absence of a curse.

Reincarnation is understood as one of the greatest means by which God assists the soul to reach his or her true destiny by giving the soul additional opportunities to grow and develop in this world so that it can earn eternal life. Receiving something for nothing is referred to in the *Zohar* as the "bread of shame." What seems to be the "curse" of Adam to have to toil to earn his livelihood is actually a hidden blessing and part of God's plan for humankind. Although in general the soul's initial inclination is to want to stay in its more pristine spiritual state in the upper worlds, God's purpose for the soul paradoxically entails earning its exalted state in this, the lowest of all worlds. Gilgul, although a means of punishment of sorts, is in essence a great kindness from God.

Therefore when we see the righteous suffer and the evil prosper we need to understand what is really happening in the big picture. We cannot fathom the exact ways these judgments occur, nor should we look at others suffering and try to figure out why they "deserve" it. Rather we should attempt to see in all occurrences in this world God's justness, especially when it comes to our own suffering. In addition, we are taught that although everyone who suffers does so for a reason, it is not our business to judge others' suffering, but rather to compassionately assist in every way we can to alleviate their pain or distress. Further, while a person's actions may be condemned, we should be careful not to condemn his essential being. We are taught this lesson in the biblical punishment of stripes given for certain infractions of the law. It is forbidden to exceed forty lashes lest our brother's standing be diminished in our eyes (Deuteronomy 25:3). Even when dispensing punishment, he is still called "brother." No matter how much we are called upon to justify God's judgments it should never be at the expense of our brother's basic humanity.

Although we will never fully understand the ways of God we are still urged to contemplate that which we can grasp. In Judaism, faith is not blind; rather it is based on knowledge. This is alluded to in the Shema, where the letters *ayin* and *dalet* (of the word "shema") are enlarged. These two letters spell out the word *da*, "witness," and when reversed spell out the word *ed*, "know." The Jewish people are faithful witnesses to God's oneness in the world, yet this mission should be based as much as possible on knowledge. There are many things about God far beyond our ability to comprehend; nevertheless we must strive to understand God's ways as best we can. This idea is expressed in the verse: "The hidden things are for Hashem, our God, and the revealed things for us and our children" (Deuteronomy 29:28). The Torah, the blueprint of creation, along with the teachings of the prophets and sages, sheds light on that which is hidden in order to reveal it as much as is humanly possible.

In the excellent book *Shoah: A Jewish Perspective on Tragedy in the Context of the Holocaust* by Rabbi Yoel Schwartz and Rabbi Yitzchak Goldstein (Brooklyn, NY: Mesorah Publications, Ltd., 1990, p. 43) there is an extremely important teaching regarding understanding God's judgments. Nachmanides explains that it is the duty of all those who serve God to investigate the fairness of God's verdicts to the best of their ability, even though we could depend on faith alone, for by doing so we come to validate that which we can understand, while acknowledging and accepting those things we cannot fathom. The book then states that a belief in the teachings of gilgul should remove all doubts regarding the righteousness of God's ways for in these secrets lie a full explanation of all that occurs to a human being.

Although the true reasons for peoples suffering or prospering may elude us, there is no doubt that suffering in general, as well as many of the most difficult situations in life, can be understood as being part of the ongoing chain of reincarnation. Therefore, many modern texts, whether Kabbalistically oriented or not, explain among other things, the death of young children, stillbirths, being born with physical defects, sudden deaths, or those who fight prolonged battles with terminal diseases, as rooted in the secrets of reincarnation. To feel one is suffering for no apparent purpose is one of the hardest and loneliest of occurrences, while extracting from suffering deep meaning and relevance is one of life's most profound and redeeming aspects.

In the same book (pp. 44–45), a beautiful parable by the Chafetz Chaim is brought to explain why one man is poor and another rich, when by external appearances the poor man does as much good as the rich man. In so doing he shows how important the understanding of reincarnation is when contemplating the true reality of life. The Chafetz Chaim compares this scenario to the instance of a traveler who comes to a synagogue in which he had never been before. The traveler notices that the men who are being called to the Torah to recite the blessings before and after each reading are being called in an apparently random order. He approaches the sexton and queries him as to why one man was being called up from those sitting on one side of the synagogue, the next from another side, and then the one after that from yet another side. He was told that since he was not a regular at this particular synagogue, he could not possibly understand the order that was being followed very carefully. The sexton then clarified for the traveler the rationale behind the order in which the men were being called.

The Chafetz Chaim explains that this is how we can understand why one individual is poor and another is rich. We see in this lifetime so little of the bigger picture that we are like the traveler to the synagogue who tries to understand what he cannot possibly understand without the true breadth of circumstances. He goes on to say that if we had truly broad vision we would see that in a previous lifetime the rich man was actually poor and the poor man was rich. Each one had experienced his particular challenges in that situation and now was being presented with the opposite circumstances so that he or she could complete their personal tikkun.

The Chafetz Chaim commented in general that now that the great teachers of Kabbalah have revealed the secrets of gilgul there is no longer any doubt to applying this wisdom to understand God's ways, especially in relation to suffering. What may initially appear as suffering may in fact be a great kindness, providing the means to a soul's purification, atonement, and rectification.

FREE WILL AND DIVINE PROVIDENCE

One of the big questions relating to reincarnation is, How can the soul have free will if it is a reincarnated soul that brings with it all the baggage from a previous lifetime? Considering the reasons why the soul has returned, in combination with the very specific repairs it is called upon to do, would seem to infringe on its ability to exercise any measure of autonomy and true choice! To understand the answer to this very important and real question we must first discuss free will and Divine Providence in general, and then apply what we learn to this specific dilemma.

When probing deeply into the nature of the world one finds paradoxes everywhere, from the spiritual realm to the modern description of reality according to the Theory of Relativity and Quantum Mechanics. God Himself is referred to as "[the One] Who carries opposites" (*Likkutei Torah* 3:68) or as "Paradox of Paradoxes" (*Teshuvot Harashba* 18). God is described similarly in a number of parables that express the mystery of Divinity and the creation, such as, "He is the place of the world, but the world is not His place" (*Genesis Rabba* 68:9) and "[He is] present yet not present" (*Sefer Hamaʾamarim* 5679; pp. 237ff.). Rabbi Akiba said, "Everything is foreseen, yet the freedom of choice is given. The world is judged in goodness and everything depends on the abundance of good deeds" (*Pirkei Avot* 3:19).

According to many commentators the greatest paradox in relation to man is that both free will and Divine Providence operate simultaneously. Most religions or philosophies tend to be inclined towards one of these options at the expense of the other, or totally negate one in favor of the other, while Torah embraces not only this paradox, but in fact all paradoxes, as reflecting a deeper and truer reflection of reality. That both free will and Divine Providence can both be true stretches the mind to comprehend that which is just beyond comprehension. Yet stretching the mind is a great exercise and gives us deeper insight into how life unfolds.

Despite Judaism's firm belief in free will, it does not function independently of other factors. Maimonides, one of the strongest proponents of the importance of free will as we have already mentioned, states clearly that if one's sins increase significantly, the gift of free will may be taken away (*Mishneh Torah, Hilchot Teshuva* 6:3). Free will is not open-ended; if one abuses his freedom of choice often enough, he may very well lose the privilege of using it.

It must also be stated that many times we think we are exercising our free will when in truth we are but reacting to a plethora of biological, psychological, emotional, and behavioral factors. The true exercise of free will is a very precious commodity and not as common as supposed. Giving into our animal natures, succumbing to peer pressure, following the crowd, and being overly influenced by society all limit the true exercise of free will.

One of the most famous of debates in the field of the social sciences was in regard to which factors most influence a person in determining his or her path in life and decision-making – nature or nurture. Do genetics rule or does one's upbringing override a person's more instinctual and inherited temperament? Yet when reflecting on this debate we see that in relation to true free will, both nature and nurture are on one side, while the ability to rise above all influencing factors and to make decisions from a truly objective outlook is on the other.

The point is that although we firmly believe in free will we need to have a more concrete and objective understanding of what it is we are talking about. This is very important regarding our original question, for as we discussed above, we are born against our will, die against our will, and are judged against our will. In other words, free choice operates within specifically defined and somewhat limited parameters. And there is no way of avoiding the many influences already mentioned above – they are a fact of life.

In a fascinating passage, the Talmud records the following pre-birth scenario: "The angel appointed over pregnancies takes a drop to the Holy One and asks Him: 'Master of the universe, what will become of this drop? Will it be strong or weak, wise or foolish, wealthy or poor?' The angel does not ask: Will it be wicked or righteous? This is in accord with the statement of Rabbi Hanina:

All is in the hands of Heaven except the fear of Heaven" (*Niddah* 16b). In another passage, the Talmud evinces a belief in "soul mates," two souls predestined for each other from before birth (*Sotah* 2a), and thus, on the surface of things, establishes yet another limiting factor in our lives. The implication of these teachings is that much of what describes a person – strong or weak, wise or foolish, rich or poor – are determined to a great extent before birth. These things depend, and are realized, through a combination of genes and the specific conditions one is born into. What is it that determines these factors, however? From a spiritual point of view they come from the particular requirements necessary for each soul to fulfill its particular purpose and rectification. And according to the teachings of reincarnation, these specific factors are determined in large measure based on one's previous lifetimes.

The predetermined circumstances into which a person is born are referred to as *mazal*, as in the Talmudic statement: "Life, children, and sustenance do not depend on merit, rather on mazal" (*Mo'ed Katan* 28a). The constellations are called *mazalot*, and infer predetermination or forces beyond our control, due to many ancient people's belief in the ruling power of the stars. Mazal comes from the root that means "flowing." One's mazal is those predetermined elements that flow to a person from Above and which give him the tools that he needs to accomplish what he needs to in life. But even so, there is a lot of leeway in the system, and nothing is definite. A person may be given every blessing and opportunity to succeed both physically and spiritually, but through his or her own lack of maturity or refinement fails miserably. Or the opposite – one may be born in the worst possible circumstances and yet succeed beyond all expectations. This is the power of free will. What we are given is predetermined, but what we do with what we are given is in our hands. This too is not so simple, as we will now see.

Although each person has his or her own particular purpose in life, the stage encompasses much more than just our own roles. Just as an individual is bound by many predetermined factors and circumstances, so too are the Jewish people and all humankind. Ever since the sin of Adam and Eve we are all bound by the consequences of the primordial exile from the Garden of Eden and the accompanying "curses." This creates the existential reality in which we live and die, the parameters over which we have no choice.

The Jewish people in particular are bound by a covenant with God and all that it entails. When God made the first covenant with Abraham at the "covenant of the pieces," He told him that his progeny would be afflicted by another nation, and in a land not their own, for four hundred years, but afterwards they would come out with great wealth (Genesis 15:1–21). This prophecy became manifest in the slavery in Egypt and the Exodus. The question becomes: what choices did the Jewish people have during those four hundred years as to their fate? Was it not all predestined?

The answer is both yes and no. On a certain level history unfolded as God had determined, but the actual way in which it did so and each person's role in that unfolding was highly fluid. This holds true in general for how Divine Providence and free will operate simultaneously. Joseph, when he finally revealed himself to his brothers, who had sold him twenty-two years earlier, said, "Therefore do not be sad nor angry with yourselves that you sold me here, for God sent me here before you in order to preserve life" (Genesis 45:5). Later, Joseph said to them, "But as for you, you thought to do me evil, while God meant it for the good..." (Genesis 50:20). Free will once again is shown to be somewhat relative. The brothers made their choices and acted accordingly, yet Joseph reveals to them that in effect they were bringing to fruition the designs of a Higher Power without realizing that they were doing so at the time. The mystifying manner in which individual choices and Divine Providence dovetail, regardless of the choices made, lies at the heart of the paradox. God is infinitely adaptable and no matter what choices a person selects, God makes sure the individual's ultimate purpose is fulfilled. This holds equally true for all humankind. When needed, God intervenes in open or hidden ways so that a person stays somewhat on the right path. Whether it takes an individual one lifetime or a hundred, is a changing variable in an accounting only God knows.

The same holds true for how long it will be till the world is ready for the Messianic era and the fulfillment of man's ultimate purpose. And here too there is a merger of free will and Divine Providence. In the book of Isaiah when speaking about the final redemption God says through the prophet, "In its time I will hasten it" (60:22). The Talmud asks: If it is in its time, meaning a set determined time, how can it be hastened? The Talmud answers: If they are deserving, it will be hastened; if not, it will be in its appointed time (*Sanhedrin* 98a). Yet, the Talmud also predicts that this cycle of history and life on earth as we know it will last six thousand years followed by the Messianic era (*Sanhedrin* 97a). Once again the line between free choice and Divine Providence are blurred.

Earlier we cited Rashi's explanation of the "fallen one" in the biblical text. The fact that this individual is destined to fall off a roof does not mean that it has to be off of your roof that he falls! History unfolds according to a dynamic set to fulfill God's ultimate plan for all of humanity. Each person in every generation plays his or her part. Every individual affects the whole, and the whole affects the individual. The very important principle – "All of Israel is responsible one for the other" (*Song of Songs Rabba* on 7:8) – is learned from the verse in Leviticus (26:37) that "they shall fall one man upon another." The Talmud explains that one man will stumble by the sin of another, thus teaching us how every Jew is responsible one for the other (*Shevuot* 39a).

The Jewish people are told repeatedly by Moses that the covenant with God entails clear rewards and punishments and unambiguous laws of cause and effect. In a classic formula of free will he puts the choice before them: "I call heaven and earth today as witnesses against you, that I have set before you life and death, blessing and curse – therefore choose life that you and your children shall live..." (Deuteronomy 30:19). And still, Moses tells the people shortly afterwards that they will in the end rebel against God, and the Torah lays out exactly how Jewish history would unfold. Anyone knowing even the basics of Jewish history can see that everything the Torah predicts has come true. This brings us back to our question as to how does individual free will operate within the strictures of a people's predestined history.

Perhaps the greatest advice on how to balance these two realities is given in *Pirkei Avot* (2:4): "Make His will your will, so that He will make your will His will. Nullify your will before His will so that He will nullify the will of others before your will." According to this wisdom our ultimate goal is that our free choice should exactly reflect His Providence.

We now take our discussion regarding free will and Divine Providence and apply it to our original question regarding reincarnation: How can we have free will if our present existence is determined by the effects of previous lifetimes?

The impact of previous *gilgulim* (pl., incarnations), as we have seen, are actually just one among a host of factors affecting a human being. Reincarnation, then, is but one of the many factors influencing a person, and just like one can either overcome or succumb to certain forces and drives in life, so too through free will one can surmount the effects of previous lifetimes, or alternatively, be stifled by the ghosts of the past.

According to the passage from the Talmud quoted above, many circumstances of a person's life are decided prior to his birth. All of these are part of the Divine judgment that certainly has taken into consideration what a person did or did not do in a previous lifetime. And even if this be the soul's inaugural venture into this world, it too comes into its earthly body with a very specific individual purpose, which is further connected to the overall plan for creation. In this sense, our freedom of choice has very defined parameters indeed, and is not as absolute as we might have thought.

A general principle of gilgul as taught from a Jewish

perspective states that despite the fact that previous lifetimes help shape the conditions of a person's life, each new lifetime is not burdened by the negative energy of a previous one. In other words, the challenges and the tikkunim that are needed to correct prior errors present themselves in each new lifetime, but the choice to actually deal with these remains ours. Even if, for example, the consequences of a previous lifetime lead us to be born poor, weak, or handicapped in some way, we still have the freedom to choose how to relate to that situation and what our attitude will be to life. It is in fact only through the granting of free choice that we could come to rectify the effects of our past. For without free will we would inevitably fall into the same mistakes as previously.

Therefore, although reincarnation does impact our lives, the negative traits, actions, or attitudes do not carry over in the sense of binding us to these old patterns of behavior from one life to another. *This is an important general principle: negativity in its essence does not transfer from lifetime to lifetime, whereas the essence of good is transmitted between lifetimes.* This is a result of God's chessed, His loving-kindness, which is reflected in the word gilgul numerically equaling chessed. Yet even the good of a previous lifetime does not guarantee that the soul will translate this into a true tikkun of the past. This still lies in the realm of free choice granted to each person, no matter their past.

Each life is considered a new beginning, a clean slate, and is judged wholly on the soul's actions in its current state. Some even consider it easier to repair mistakes from the past, since distance from the intellectual and emotional confusion and turmoil that caused the original blemishes makes it more conducive for the soul to fix that which is in need of repair.

Judaism emphasizes the uniqueness, purpose, and importance of each individual and the critical role of free choice in shaping one's destiny. The whole point of gilgul is not to be bound by the past, but to elevate oneself beyond all obstacles in the present. Even though a soul may return many times to this world, it is never exactly the same soul, and it is certainly not the same body.

Therefore despite an obvious link between lifetimes, it is a totally new combination of soul-and-body dynamics at play.

Just as free will operates in some mysterious way simultaneously with Divine Providence, similarly an individual soul with free will operates within the strictures of reincarnation and the many other forces of the past which shape its present. Along with our individual fate and destiny, we are all connected in one way or another to God's plan for creation as a whole. This is especially pertinent for the Jewish people who are bound to God by an everlasting covenant and a specific mission in the world, as will be discussed further in Chapter Five.

REFLECTING ON REINCARNATION

An important question is raised concerning how important it is to know and how much effort should be expended in trying to uncover previous lifetimes. The Arizal not only revealed the inner teachings relating to gilgul but was known to tell people their previous lifetimes and the specific tikkunim needed in this world. Many people, including great scholars and students of Kabbalah, approached the Arizal for this information.

The Ba'al Shem Tov, on the other hand, despite his leading role in spreading the teachings regarding reincarnation, felt it less important in his day to know one's specific soul history. His overall emphasis, as discussed in Chapter One, was hashra'ah, direct experience of God. For this reason he felt that unless there was an immediate and tangible benefit from knowing one's previous lifetimes, this information could possibly confuse or cause difficulties for a person psychologically and emotionally. Therefore despite the fact that the Ba'al Shem Tov was known to reveal to people their soul history, he only did so when he felt there was an immediate and beneficial reason.

This idea is still sound advice today, especially when many modern therapists and psychologists use hypnosis and deep relaxation as part of past life regression therapy. There seems to be no doubt that remembering past lives is possible using such methods, but there is also the constant danger that these techniques could bring out all kinds of other memories or associations from a host of sources that may be confused with real past lifetimes. Therefore one should keep in mind the Ba'al Shem Tov's advice in this matter.

It is also very important to point out that one's previous lifetimes are not felt on the conscious plane; rather their effect is on the more subconscious levels of the psyche. Except in very rare cases, a person is not aware at all of his or her previous lives, or of the specific reasons for incarnating at this time in this body. Only when delving deeply into the unconscious realms of the soul are we able to begin to contact these previous lifetimes.

According to Rabbi Yitzchak Ginsburgh, when probing the subterranean strata of the unconscious, one does not have to have prophetic powers to unearth previous lifetimes, rather it is sufficient to be aware that by delving into the fears, phobias, and wounds found deep inside, one is contacting remnants of prior incarnations as well (Yitzchak Ginsburgh, *Transforming Darkness into Light* [Jerusalem: Gal Einai, 2002], p. 142). The specifics of the past are less important than dealing with the effects of these deeply rooted feelings in the present. The repairs needed in this life are set in motion by the past but are not hostage to it. Healing lies in recognizing the spiritual work to be done in the here and now and then actually doing it. Each person deep inside has an intuitive knowledge of what they need to do to realize their potential and correct what they need to in order to live a life of meaning and purpose. Of course, acting on that deep knowledge entails courage, fortitude, and commitment.

We are taught in the Talmud that when a fetus is in its mother's womb an angel comes and teaches it the entire Torah, but at the moment of birth the angel touches the baby on the cleft of its lip and he or she forgets it all (*Niddah* 30b). The obvious question is, why teach the fetus the entire Torah only to cause him or her to forget it? Although the newborn forgets the Torah on a conscious level, he or she has this wisdom indelibly etched on the unconscious where it serves as a deep reminder of what is right and wrong, and impresses a memory of the lofty level of the soul to which, by all rights, it can return.

Other primordial memories are likewise engraved in the unconscious layers of the soul The experience of the sublime spiritual state of the soul as it existed in the upper worlds before it descended into a body is imbedded in the deepest recesses of consciousness. That pristine memory of being in the presence of God is alluded to in the verse, "God, before Whom I stood" (1 Kings 17:1, 18:5; 2 Kings 3:14, 5:16). The soul as well has the deeply ingrained memory of hearing God command it to descend into a body where it is charged to fulfill its specific purpose and mission.

All these primal memories are impressed upon the soul as road signs directing the soul towards its ultimate purpose. This idea relates to our previous lives as well. Their vague memory is buried in the deeper levels of consciousness in order to assist those willing to do the serious spiritual work of soul refinement. For this reason the Ba'al Shem Tov would first initiate a new student into the more inner aspects of his own soul by asking him, "What do you remember?"

This, then, is where prayer and teshuva come into the picture. Prayer is one of the most potent spiritual exercises for both experiencing the presence of God and for exploring the soul's deeper levels. These experiences can take place in both formal and informal prayer. Also, practices such as song, meditation, visualization, and being in nature are powerful aids in the experience of prayer. This is why the Ba'al Shem Tov emphasized these various practices as part of his teachings stressing direct experience of God. For one desiring to understand the exact nature of the soul, its essential history, and its purpose and true destiny, there is perhaps no better strategy than including prayer and its accompanying practices as an ongoing spiritual discipline.

Along with prayer, the commitment to do teshuva is essential for the soul's true rectification. By teshuva we mean not only the commitment to continually assess one's thoughts, speech, and actions to insure that they are in tune with the Torah and the will of God, but even more, to be dedicated to drawing ever closer to God in love and awe. The soul at its very essence desires to unite with God. Prayer and teshuva, along with Torah study, fulfilling God's commandments, and acts of kindness, draw the presence of God continually into our lives.

When digging into the hidden canyons of the psyche one can experience not only previous lives, but can reach back even farther to one's specific soul root, and even back to the origin of the soul in the all-inclusive soul of Adam. The deeper one goes into the unconscious the more one contacts the collective unconscious of the Jewish people and all humanity. At such depths of soul essential rectifications occur that dramatically change one's present consciousness and, in a ripple effect, influence all reality.

CHAPTER FOUR:

Dynamics of Reincarnation

Now that we have traced the development of reincarnation in Jewish thought from its explicit and implied origins in the written and oral Torah, as well as in Kabbalistic texts, and we have also discussed a broader context for our subject through its varied corollaries and associated concepts, we now turn our attention to the specific system of gilgul as revealed by the Arizal.

During the many years that the Arizal spent learning in isolation in a small shack along the banks of the Nile River, he focused his studies on the *Zohar*, the classic text of Kabbalah. It is said that he would delve into the very depths of each word until he could extract its full meaning on a myriad of levels and would not proceed until reaching that elevated level of understanding. In this way he was able to reveal the inner dimensions of the *Zohar*, which till then had not been fully comprehended or appreciated. It further allowed him to develop his innovative approach to many areas of Jewish thought, including his insights into our own subject.

As the Arizal developed ideas initially revealed in the *Zohar*, he was aided by the guidance of Elijah the Prophet, who was sent to study with him. The Arizal was not only privileged to perceive new levels of the Kabbalistic tradition and to receive new revelations from on High, but was also given the permission to reveal these secrets. Many times during Jewish history great sages or mystics were aware of many Divine secrets, but because of the state of the world and the exile of the Jewish people they were not given permission to reveal them. When a tzaddik reveals secrets before their appropriate time it actually has an opposite, negative effect, which leads to tension and dissonance instead of the positive outcome it was intended to achieve.

The Arizal told his students that the secrets he was now revealing were due to new lights being revealed in the upper worlds. These lights, he taught, were the beginning stages of the Messianic era. This was in keeping with what is taught in the *Zohar* (3:124b) about the Messianic era being profoundly tied to the revelation of the inner dimensions of the Torah.

The primary area in which the Arizal demonstrated his own level of *ruach hakodesh*, "Divine inspiration," and prophetic powers was in his novel approach to the subject of gilgulim. Not only did his teachings in this area revolutionize Jewish thought, but he was known to reveal to people their past lives and the specific tikkunim they needed to perform in order to repair their souls. It is said that by merely looking at someone's forehead the Arizal could see a person's every blemish in this life and in all previous lives, and he could perceive their soul root as well.

Although the dynamics of reincarnation taught by the Arizal are primarily found in the *Gate of Reincarnations*, one of the eight volumes of his teachings organized by his primary student, Rabbi Chaim Vital, elements can be found spread throughout his teachings. They are highly complex and need much study and thought to absorb their full meaning. A full, in-depth treatment of every nuance of this intricate system is beyond the parameters of this work, nevertheless we will attempt to bring to the reader a basic outline in order that the general scope and the basic workings of reincarnation as taught by the Arizal can be comprehended.

One final point needs to be expressed before delving into this material. We have already mentioned in our introduction the difficulty one may encounter when first learning the specific dynamics of reincarnation according to the Arizal. It is not only the complexity of the matter but the way reincarnation actually works that may strain the imagination or overwhelm a logical mind unfamiliar with these ideas. Therefore the reader is urged to keep an open mind and be willing to give the ideas at hand sufficient thought.

FIVE LEVELS OF RECTIFICATION

Reincarnation, as we discussed in Chapter Two, plays itself out in the overall context of judgment. Each and every soul when it leaves this world is obliged to account for its every action, speech, and thought. This review is primarily designed to assist the soul, specifically through its own efforts, reach its ultimate goal of becoming a perfected "image of God." Therefore when this goal is achieved it is all the sweeter in that it was not a gift but was earned through hard work, sweat, and tears.

Inasmuch as each soul is unique, it comes into this world with a distinctive task and is thus judged according to its level and its mission. This was a major emphasis of the Arizal – judgment is relative and depends on many factors. A person is tried according to what stage of soul development he or she has reached – and just as important – in accordance with his or her soul history (*Gate of Reincarnations*, 6). The Ba'al Shem Tov also placed great emphasis on this principle.

Although sometimes it is within our ability to understand God's judgments, in many or even most cases it is beyond the comprehension of man. Yet we are guided by trust and the idea that all that God does is just and all that He does is for the good. According to the Arizal, the only true understanding of why certain things happen to people is based on comprehending the mechanics of gilgul.

In order to reach the elevated level of being an "image of God," the soul must go through numerous trials, and many lifetimes. In the twenty-first section of the *Gate of Reincarnations* it is explained how teshuva has the power to rectify a wrongdoing in the present, thus effectively mitigating the need for returning. But if one does not do teshuva, that soul may very well be sentenced to enter this world again in order to rectify the misdeed. In order that "no one is lost to Him" the soul is given the chance to fix things in another lifetime.

Rabbi Yitzchak Ginsburgh explains that there are actually five different levels on which judgment, punishment, and rectification occur when necessary after death. Each one is meant to instruct and rehabilitate the soul. The first three emanate more from the side of *gevurah*, "strictness," while the final two are more from the side of chessed, "loving-kindness."

The first level is *chibbut hakever*, the death pangs of the grave. Once the soul is separated from the body immediately following death, it is still very connected to the body and lingers in the vicinity. This is why burial of the body is painful for the soul. And this is why we can appreciate what it means when the Talmud states that those living in the Land of Israel and those who die on the day preceding Shabbat are spared from these travails. It also states that those who are generous in giving charity, who listen to rebuke, do acts of kindness, welcome guests into their home, and pray with intent are also spared these travails, even if they live outside the Land of Israel. These acts all elevate the soul and serve as a salve to reduce and perhaps even to eliminate the pain felt at the moment at which it separates from the body. In general, the more refined a soul is, the less pain is experienced.

The second type of tikkun is termed *kaf hakela*, a slingshot effect. It is taught in the *Zohar* that our good deeds in this world create a vapor or wind, while our bad deeds also create a vapor or wind. When the soul leaves the body these winds surround it. If the winds have come about because of his good deeds, they defend him. If, however, they were brought about by evil deeds, they thrust his soul around to and fro, like being slung from a slingshot. In this way the soul experiences the unsettled feeling of its own wrongdoing and the direct effects of its actions.

The third level originating on the side of gevurah is *gehenom*, commonly translated as "hell," but better translated as "purgatory." Rather than the eternal flames of damnation described in Christian theology, gehenom in Jewish thought is a period of intense soul purification for specific misdeeds; a learning process for a limited period of time. Once the soul is purified, or purged, it moves on.

The soul's experience of "heaven" or "hell" in Jewish tradition is greatly influenced by a person's actions in this world and is in great measure a direct product of man's own making. Although it states in the Talmud that fire is one sixtieth of gehenom, the way the soul experiences the fires of gehenom is in good measure a result of the unbridled and un-rectified flames of passion experienced in this world and the heat of shame when the soul faces its own failures and weaknesses.

Fire, as viewed by Jewish law, has the power to purify impurities in vessels and likewise has the power to cleanse the soul. Suffering, when related to properly, can be used as a great force for atonement and rectification, propelling the soul forward. One could even say that passing through gehenom has a certain advantage in that it mitigates the need to return to this world so many times. Despite the relative strictness of the first three levels of tikkun, they are all meant to bring the soul to its ultimate state of perfection.

The next two levels of repair of the soul emanate more from the side of chessed. The first one is termed ibbur, which literally means "impregnation." Discussed briefly in Chapter One, this idea plays a major part in the Arizal's system. The Arizal explains that a soul may enter the body of another for a limited time for two reasons: in order to "fix" itself by participating in the positive actions of the host soul, or alternatively, in order to assist the host soul accomplish what it cannot do on its own. In both cases the person who is "impregnated" with a soul is totally unconscious of this reality, although he may feel it on some level as an increase in his strength, inspiration, or motivation. The Arizal understands the well-known Talmudic axiom (*Shabbat* 104a) that if one desires to purify himself they assist him from Above, as referring to ibbur, where the impregnated soul becomes the manner in which help is sent from on High.

Whatever the reason for ibbur, it is deemed a great chessed from God as it helps one in need and allows a departed soul the chance to elevate itself without having to reincarnate for an entire lifetime. It is obvious that this concept has wide-ranging implications, which will be discussed at greater length later.

The final and highest level of rectification is gilgul, whose numerical value is 72, equaling chessed. It is interesting to note that the word gehenom equals 108, exactly 1½ times the value of gilgul. Rabbi Ginsburgh explains that this relationship, referred to in Kabbalah as *shalem vachetzi*, "a whole and a half," appears in numerous places throughout the Bible, and indicates a deep intrinsic connection between words and concepts.

Both gehenom and gilgul begin with the letter gimmel, which, as we saw in Chapter Two, represents dispensing reward and punishment. Gehenom (108) equals both chessed and gilgul (the numerical value of each being 72) plus another half (36), indicating an intense alternative to gilgul. In other words, it is a great chessed on God's part to allow a soul to rectify itself through gilgul, rather than the more intense experience of gehenom. As long as a soul progresses somewhat it is allowed to return in gilgul; if not, it must experience gehenom, which itself is a type of chessed.

Rabbi Ginsburgh further explains that in modern science the various particles within the atom are all assigned a measure according to their rate of rotation or spin. All the matter particles have a spin equal to the electron, equaling ½ spin, while all the nongravitational force or energy carriers have a spin of 1. This relationship, reproduced in every atom and at every level of physical reality, is the same ratio as shalem vachetzi, "a whole and a half."

Gilgul, Rabbi Ginsburgh teaches, relates to the higher levels of soul energy and rehabilitation (corresponding to spin 1), while gehenom relates more to cleansing the soul for its overindulgence in those areas connected to the body and matter (corresponding to spin ½). When gilgul is no longer sufficient to rectify a soul due to its excess attachment to physical material, an additional ½ is needed to readjust the relationship of the soul to matter.

Although the Arizal does teach that the study of Torah shields a person from gehenom, this is understood to be referring to a very high level of study not attainable by most people, as it is clear from many different source texts that even men who do study Torah may have to experience gehenom in order to rectify certain parts of their soul. Those, however, who are indeed on a very high level of Torah study would be left with only reincarnation as the means with which to repair the soul. From here we see that gilgul is certainly looked upon as a Godly expression of chessed. For a tzaddik, gilgul is not just a chance for tikkun; it also allows the possibility of achieving ever higher levels of refinement for the soul, as it goes from "strength to strength" (Psalms 84:8).

REASONS FOR REINCARNATION

The opening sections of the *Gate of Reincarnations* deal primarily with an explanation of the five levels of the soul, as taught in Kabbalah and Chassidut: *nefesh*, *ruach*, *neshama*, *chaya*, and *yechida*. Each name refers to an ascending hierarchy of soul powers, and serves as a powerful tool in analyzing and understanding the human psyche.

Nefesh, the lowest level of the soul, refers to what is commonly termed the animal soul, the instinctual and behavioral drives and patterns of human action most associated with the body. *Ruach*, or "spirit," relates to the emotions; *neshama*, the inner soul, is considered the seat of the intellect; *chaya*, "the living one," refers to the interaction between consciousness and its superconscious origin; and *yechida*, "the single, unique one," relates to the Divine aspect of soul.

The Arizal explains that a soul, in order to complete itself, must perfect all five levels. One does not receive the next level of soul in the fullest sense until he perfects the preceding level. As can be imagined, this process can take many lifetimes. As each level of soul reaches a rectified state it is able to receive the next ascending level. This continues till all levels of soul are complete. In more simple terms, the Arizal was teaching that for a soul to reach completion it must clarify and rectify its instinctual, emotional, and intellectual levels of consciousness, along with its higher levels of innate spiritual and divine consciousness.

The system of the Arizal contains many general rules and numerous exceptions as well. When a soul first comes to this world it has the opportunity to rectify all the levels of soul in one lifetime. The nefesh enters at the time of birth, the ruach at age thirteen, and the neshama at age twenty. The Arizal does not mention when it is that the two highest levels enter the soul as these are its most elusive and transcendent strata, and are only reached after much spiritual toil and with Divine assistance. If it is not able to rectify all these levels in its first lifetime and instead blemishes them, in subsequent lifetimes it will only be able to repair one level at a time. Once each level is fixed, it must die and then come back again to fix the next level.

If a soul merits for example to receive its ruach and neshama after its nefesh is rectified, but then blemishes its ruach and neshama, its rectified nefesh will only be able to return in collusion with another soul, while its blemished ruach and neshama will incarnate into different people in its next lifetime. When all levels of soul are rectified they may once again unite in one person.

Sometimes, the Arizal explains, the various parts of a person's soul will be rooted in different "worlds" or spiritual levels (as will be explained shortly), each one on a different phase of soul development. This idea along with numerous other details of the system he revealed correspond in a striking manner to many ideas presented in modern psychology for understanding the complex forces at work in the human psyche. Various conscious and unconscious imbalances, tendencies, drives, and phobias as described by current psychological analysis have their parallels in the various descriptions of the Arizal concerning the complexity of the soul in general, and the constellation of forces present in an individual due to reincarnation, in particular.

The soul can be likened to an inverted iceberg. An iceberg has a tiny fraction of its mass protruding above the water, while the vast majority lies undetected below the surface. (This same explanation could be used to describe the relationship between the conscious and unconscious.) The soul is similar, but inverted: the vast majority of the soul remains rooted above and undetected, while only a small fraction actually manifests itself within the body. As an individual begins to clarify his or her self it draws down into this world higher and higher levels of soul, which then have their opportunity to fully rectify themselves. In Kabbalah, a similar metaphor is given by using the image of a tree instead of an iceberg. The roots of a tree are hidden and below the surface, while the trunk and branches are above, whereas for the soul the opposite is true – its roots remain hidden above and its manifestation, the trunk and branches, are below.

Rabbi Yitzchak Ginsburgh compares this reality to genes and genetic traits that lie dormant and hidden in one generation and appear in the next. This reflects the very important general principle that it is never the exact same soul that incarnates in a new life; rather, there are always new aspects of the soul which are not revealed in one life, but which become manifest in the next lifetime.

Understanding these teachings helps explain how people seem to be so vastly different even from a young age, some being child prodigies – the *Zohar* speaks, for example, of the child wonder, the *yenuka*, who comes into this world with an elevated soul and high level of maturity – while others are mentally, physically, or spiritually challenged. It also goes a long way to explaining how one person can have so many varying and, at times, contradictory attributes and attitudes.

Another important principle taught by the Arizal is that those levels of the soul that have reached completion or perfection need never return, while only those levels of soul still needing perfection incarnate. Although the soul which returns has aspects of the previous soul, it only incarnates in combination with other souls or different levels of its own soul, as will be explained in the continuation of this chapter. This is not an easy concept to absorb but when properly integrated brings us to an entirely new grasp of what actually comprises an individual soul.

Along with completing the five levels discussed above, the Arizal taught that these levels of soul must each rise through four worlds as taught in Kabbalah: *Assiyah*, the World of "Action," *Yetzirah*, the World of "Formation," *Beriah*, the World of "Creation," and *Atzilut*, the World of "Emanation." Atzilut, the World of "Emanation," is closest to its infinite Divine source and each succeeding world represents a more condensed material manifestation of God's pure light. Depending on which world a soul is rooted in defines its basic orientation and response to our highly physical and mundane world, the World of "Action." There is, according to the Arizal, a fifth even higher world, called *Adam Kadmon*, "Primordial Man." These five worlds correspond directly to the five levels of soul in the following manner:

Kabbalistic World	Level of Soul
Adam Kadmon – Primordial Man	Yechida – unique Divine soul
Atzilut – Emanation	Chaya – "living one"
Beriah – Creation	Neshama – intellectual
Yetzirah – Formation	Ruach – emotional
Assiyah – Action	Nefesh – instinctual

Each level of soul actually contains all five levels, known in Kabbalistic terminology as the principle of "inter-inclusion." In order to reach its complete fulfillment each soul must rectify all five levels of soul in each of the five worlds. Despite this incredible complexity, the Arizal not only could identify which levels of a person's soul needed fixing, but also in which world the various levels of soul had their source. According to this model we can imagine how complex the soul truly is and therefore its tikkun and perfection are likewise multifaceted, and need much clarification and effort through many lifetimes. In general, if one merits rectifying his or her nefesh, ruach, and neshama, that soul no longer needs to incarnate. The higher levels of chaya and yechida are reached only by rare and great souls. These souls may continue to incarnate, not so much because of any verdict against them or needed repair, but to further elevate their souls or to assist others in reaching their potential.

In the relatively short eighth section of the *Gate of Reincarnations*, a number of general reasons are given as to why people must return to this world. In other sections these relatively simple ideas are expanded upon in great detail. First, it states, a person reincarnates because of a sin or sins committed in a previous lifetime. Second, a person returns to this world in order to complete his soul by performing a mitzvah (or mitzvot) he failed to do or did not do with the proper focus. Third, one may return to this world to influence others and assist them in their personal tikkunim.

Further, the Arizal states, one may return in order to come together with his or her soul mate, either because he or she did not merit to unite with his or her other half in a previous incarnation, or alternatively, two soul mates did come together, but because of certain sins they committed they need to return together in order to rectify what was previously blemished.

Intrinsically tied to the teaching that each soul needs to rectify and clarify all five levels of soul is the teaching of the Arizal that this is done specifically through the study of Torah and the fulfillment of the 613 mitzvot (*Gate of Reincarnations*, 11 & 16). The mitzvot are divided into 248 positive mitzvot, to which correspond the 248 organs of the body, and the 365 negative mitzvot, to which correspond the 365 tendons or sinews. These 613 mitzvot and their correspondence in the human body are further connected to the soul itself, which has a "body" consisting of 613 "organs," the spiritual complement of the 613 parts of the body. By performing the 248 positive mitzvot and guarding oneself from transgressing the prohibitions of the 365 negative mitzvot, the soul is enclothed fully in the 613 mitzvot, allowing it to reach its full and consummate state. In turn, this level of spiritual attainment then filters down into the 613 corresponding parts of the body.

The Arizal goes on to teach how each mitzvah needs to be fulfilled properly in thought, speech, and action, as well as on the various levels of PARDES, an acronym symbolizing the four basic strata of interpreting the Torah (*Gate of Reincarnations*, 17). Beginning from below and building up, the P corresponds to *peshat*, the literal meaning; R represents *remez*, the hinted to, or alluded to, meaning; D stands for *derash*, the homiletic or allegorical meaning; and the S corresponds to *sod*, the secret or Kabbalistic meaning.

There are many mitzvot which cannot be observed today due to the lack of a Temple, King, or Sanhedrin, "high court." However, according to the midrash (*Vayikra Rabba* 7:3), these can still be fulfilled through proper study. If they are given the appropriate consideration in one's learning, says the Arizal, then one will not have to be reincarnated to actually observe them. But other mitzvot that one lacks is a reason for reincarnation; although sometimes returning in ibbur to perform these mitzvot along with the host soul is sufficient.

It is explained in Kabbalah and Chassidut that many times a person will be drawn to keep, and will place great emphasis on, one or more mitzvot in particular. It is very likely that these mitzvot are among those especially needed for that soul's tikkun, perhaps from a previous lifetime. Alternatively, for one who feels weak or deficient in a certain mitzvah, this may be a sign that it is exactly in this area that spiritual work needs to be done in order to rectify a present lacking, or one emanating from a past lifetime.

The crucial point is that mitzvot are far more than actions we are arbitrarily commanded to perform. They are, instead, powerful agents through which one can repair and elevate the soul. In this sense mitzvot, along with the study of Torah, are the main vehicle through which a Jew completes the perfection of his or her soul. For a non-Jew this is accomplished through fulfilling the seven Noachide laws incumbent on all humankind.

While it is clear that transgressing one of the 365 prohibitions will blemish the soul, the Arizal noted that in a similar, but to a lesser degree, not performing one of the positive mitzvot also leaves a blemish on the soul that needs to be corrected in a future gilgul. One case which illustrates this point and is mentioned by the Arizal is someone who did not merit having children in one lifetime must reincarnate to try again in another.

It states in *Pirkei Avot* (4:3): "Do not be scornful of any person and do not be disdainful of anything, for you have no person without his hour and no thing without its place." The Ba'al Shem Tov expounded that a person can live in this world for seventy years just to be able to fulfill one single mitzvah or take one simple action. This is their hour. Although the mitzvah may appear to be minor it may be just the deed required to complete a certain level of soul. More likely though, is the example of a person who seriously stumbles in one life at a climactic moment and is given a chance in another lifetime to rectify it. It is as if one's whole life had led up to this moment. Maimonides wrote that one can measure the success of teshuva if one makes a correct choice in the exact same situation wherein he previously failed. Kabbalah teaches that this teshuva transcends lifetimes.

We see then that a soul may need to reincarnate for that which it did wrong or for that which it has yet to do right, and even for what he did right but in a superficial manner. Rabbi Shlomo Carlebach taught that there are two types of teshuva – for those things we have done wrong and for those things we did right, but in a perfunctory or unenthusiastic way. Further, we see that sometimes a soul returns to this world to help itself, while at other times to help others. And it may, by returning to help others, in the end actually help itself.

THEREFORE GOD DOES ALL THESE THINGS

Of all the verses in the Torah that have been interpreted to allude to the dynamics of gilgul perhaps none is as important as (Job 33:29): "Thus God does all these things twice or three times with a man, to bring back his soul from the pit, to be enlightened with the light of the living." The Arizal perceived in these words multiple layers of meaning, which serve to explain many variants in the actual mechanics of reincarnation (*Gate of Reincarnations*, 5).

The first layer of meaning interprets the words, "two or three times," to mean that a soul has up to three times to attempt to rectify itself. The idea that a soul is given three chances by God but not a fourth is also derived from a verse quoted by Rabbi Yosi bar Yehuda in the Talmud: A man who transgresses one time is forgiven, a second time is forgiven, a third time is forgiven, a fourth time is not forgiven, as it is said, "Thus says God: 'Three of Israel's sins [I have already pardoned], but for the fourth, I will not let him go unpunished' (Amos 2:6), and it is said, 'Thus God does all these things twice or three times with a man, to bring back his soul from the pit, to be enlightened with the light of the living'" (*Yoma* 86b). Although the simple meaning of this statement in the Talmud relates to events within one lifetime, the Arizal explained it as applying equally to the dynamics of gilgul. He also revealed a concept called *gilgul bachayim*, a "reincarnation in [the same] life," when a person who does teshuva is transformed to such an extent he or she is considered a new person. It is as if they have reincarnated in the same lifetime, thus giving them an opportunity to continue rectifying higher soul levels without having to pass away. It is stated in the Talmud that one who keeps Shabbat according to its laws will be forgiven, even if he worshipped idols as in the generation of Enosh (*Shabbat* 118b). The Slonimer Rebbe explains that since this person has changed to such an extent and has abandoned his old ways he is treated like a new person.

Rabbi Yitzchak Ginsburgh teaches that the first person thought to have undergone gilgul bachayim was Abraham. After complaining to God that he had no children to continue the spiritual work he was doing, God "took him outside" (Genesis 15:5) to show him the stars and assure him that his progeny would be as numerous. The simple explanation cited by Rashi is that God revealed Himself to Abraham in his tent and then "took him outside" under the stars to make His promise to him in a dramatic way. Rashi continues by saying that God told Abraham to "go outside" your astrological calculations which tell you that you will not have children. Indeed, Abram (his name at the time of the revelation) will not have children, but Abraham will. Later God adds the letter *hei* to Abram's name (making it Abraham), denoting not just a change of name, but a qualitative change of his essential nature. This type of total transformation is what the Arizal referred to as gilgul bachayim. Rashi finishes his comments on the verse by offering another interpretation of the words "took him outside." God, in a prophetic way, raised Abram above the stars, allowing him to look down upon his condition from an entirely new and exalted perspective. This as well symbolizes the change in consciousness associated with gilgul bachayim.

This last idea is one many people can relate to. Sometimes we change directions in life so radically that it feels as if we really are a new person, as our present reality is so dramatically different than our previous lifestyle. This sense of estrangement only intensifies as the years go by, so much so that at times we can hardly remember or relate to our "previous life."

The Arizal elaborates on the theme of gilgul bachayim by saying it may also occur between two people in the same lifetime through a transfer of a part of the soul from one to another. One example cited by the Arizal for this phenomenon is the deep soul connection between David and Jonathan, as expressed in many verses in the Book of Samuel. The connection between people can be so strong until a portion of one's soul not only clings to, but merges with, the other's (*Gate of Reincarnations*, 3).

In an associated idea, it is said that just as one may experience gilgul bachayim, one may also go through kaf hakela, the feeling of being thrust about as if from a slingshot, in this life as discussed above. The feeling of transience and impermanence that marks so much of modern life can have the same effect as kaf hakela, one of the five types of tikkunim after death. If one has the right attitude towards the events which fill his or her life, then each experience can be transformed into a tikkun, as that is its intended purpose.

The Arizal further learns from our verse in Job that as long as there is some progress during one's first three incarnations a soul is given up to a thousand times to incarnate in order to rectify and elevate its soul. But if there is no progress whatsoever or a marked descent into evil after three lifetimes, then the punishment is that the nefesh is "cut off from its people," a punishment mentioned numerous times in the Torah. What this means is that the evil present in the lower soul, the nefesh, is "cut off," meaning it will never return to this world and will not be able to rise at the time of the resurrection of the dead, but since "neither does God take away life but devises means that none is lost to Him" (2 Samuel 14:14), the higher levels of soul are still given further chances to redeem themselves.

Additionally, the Arizal learned from this verse that if after three attempts a soul has not made progress, it loses its chance to incarnate into this world and must experience gehenom, as that is the only way to purify it. (In the previous example, in which a soul is "cut off," it is due to the nefesh becoming unredeemable, in contrast to this case where the lower soul is still able to be purified.) However, even if a soul must be purified through the experience of gehenom, whatever good it did accomplish also receives its reward, as God "desires goodness." On the other hand, a soul that continually attempts to improve itself, even if it is far from perfect, will be given a thousand chances to return in order to reach its goal, as alluded to at the end of our verse: "to be enlightened with the light of the living." This helps us understand not only gilgul, but also all five types of tikkun mentioned above. God's intent is for the soul to earn its exalted potential as an "image of God," and all the different levels of tikkun are the means provided through which it can attain that goal, in order that "none is lost to Him."

Another aspect of the dynamic of reincarnation learned from the verse in Job is based on a literal translation of "two or three times" as "two, three," or "two times three," meaning that if a soul does not rectify itself after one set of three attempts it is given another set of three attempts, as long as progress is being made.

The Arizal derived from the words, "with a man," that the first three times a soul incarnates it does so by itself, but if it is not able to fully rectify itself through its own power then it only incarnates "with a man," meaning with another soul, or souls, in order to gain their assistance. He also points out that "with a man" can mean through ibbur as well. This is what we have discussed a number of times already: that a person can be comprised of a number of different souls simultaneously. Thus, from the words, "two, three, with a man," the Arizal listed seven possibilities for one body:

1. a new soul in its first appearance in a body
2. an old soul; after the soul has been to this world once, it is called "old" upon its return a second time
3. an old and a new soul together
4. two old souls together
5. three old souls
6. one new and two old souls
7. three old and one new soul

It is worthwhile mentioning again that the Arizal's teachings on our subject are parallel in a striking manner to modern psychology's treatment of the highly complex and multi-layered nature of the human psyche, although their terms and language may appear to be worlds apart. The same apparent discrepancies can be said to exist in many other areas of secular knowledge and science in relation to Torah. Yet scores of books have been written in the past twenty-five years by those who have their feet firmly planted in both the secular and Torah worlds, which have not only closed the gap between the two, but have shown profound similarities between them in many respects. Although a full and in-depth analysis of the similarities and convergence of psychology and Jewish teachings on reincarnation is beyond the scope of this book, it is a fascinating subject that should and most likely will be developed.

Another insight is that a soul incarnates up to three times "with a man," or as the Arizal puts it, is enclothed in a human body. Afterwards, it is possible to return in a lower life form, or even in an inanimate object, to fix damage done by certain sins. And, as noted earlier, not all levels of soul need incarnate into these lower forms, only the specific level in need of that particular repair. In that case, the lower form somehow corresponds to the specific sin, and through this experience comes to realize its mistaken ways and is thus repaired.

One difference between being reborn in a human body and coming back in a lower life form is that when incarnating as a human there is no conscious recollection of previous lives. It is only through deep meditation or by properly interpreting one's conditions in life that we may become aware of what repairs are needed to fix misdeeds of previous lifetimes. However, if a soul returns in the form of an animal, plant, or inanimate object, the spark of soul present in that form is painfully aware of its current state and why it is where it is, and so it yearns to complete its *tikkun* in order to gain release from its lowly existence.

The Arizal taught, for example, that for the three major sins of idol worship, murder, and adultery, a soul may incarnate into an animal. Those that sin with their speech may return in rocks. Eating unfit, non-kosher foods may result in being born as a dog.

In ancient times and even today a *shochet*, "ritual slaughterer," according to Kabbalah, should have the intention of elevating any soul that may have descended into the animal he is about to ritually slaughter. This was considered one of the secrets of bringing animal sacrifices at the time of the Temple. We are likewise taught in Kabbalah and Chassidut that when we eat meat or fish we should have in mind that it may be an opportunity to elevate an incarnated soul and help them achieve some level of tikkun. This is accomplished by consuming the life force of the animal and transforming it into energy that allows us to perform mitzvot. Truly, this intent should accompany all of our acts of eating, as we are encouraged to uplift the soul or the Divine animating spark contained in our food, thereby transforming lower forms of energy into higher levels of consciousness, and ultimately into positive action.

UNDERSTANDING SOUL ROOTS

One of the key concepts relating to the dynamics of reincarnation revealed by the Arizal is that of soul roots. Although the idea seems fairly simple and straightforward, it is really quite complex. Perhaps the easiest manner in which to approach the concept is by contemplating our own family tree for a moment. Tracing our origins back to our parents is fairly simple for most of us, and not only on an emotional and psychological level, but also through our shared genetic matter. This connection between individuals holds equally true horizontally, i.e., between siblings. Further, many individuals have contact with their grandparents, and some even with their great-grandparents. As we continue to contemplate this tree we see that it includes an extended family of aunts and uncles, cousins, nephews, and nieces. Our sphere of influence also incorporates our friends with whom we feel a strong bond.

For a Jew, there should additionally be the awareness that he or she belongs to a bigger, tribal family. Looking at the big picture, one's individual family line is like a single branch on a huge tree which represents our entire people. Reaching further, every human being can trace their lineage back to Noah, his three sons, and their wives, who repopulated the world after the flood. Taking another step back in time, we come to realize how all of humanity ultimately originates with Adam and Eve. Some even trace the root of all souls back to Adam before Eve was separated from him.

We can understand how things can be traced back to one common source by analyzing and thinking about a few other related examples. Science now postulates that the current expanding universe of hundreds of billions of galaxies was all included in a singular point of matter that exploded in what is referred to as the Big Bang. This cosmological premise confirms what the sages taught: that everything that would ever be created was already present in potential on the first day of creation. We receive confirmation of this idea from another example in nature. A single seed gives birth to a tree which produces abundant seeds, many of which become viable trees that eventually produce their own seed, which in turn become trees, yet all are ultimately connected back to the first seed.

In a complementary scenario, tracing soul roots can be compared to various scientific studies which take a living organism or entity of matter and analyze it in ever smaller units or frames of reference. What appears on the surface to be relatively simple thus turns out to be unfathomably complex. Even atoms and cells have turned out to be so intricate that new discoveries are made constantly. Each time scientists think they have thoroughly analyzed the smallest component it is revealed that these are made up of even smaller constituent parts.

In like fashion, the Arizal explains in phenomenal detail how all souls that would ever be born were included in Adam. He first takes the framework discussed above where the body and soul are composed of 613 components – 248 organs and 365 sinews, corresponding to the 248 positive mitzvot and the 365 prohibitive mitzvot respectively – and describes how every soul is connected to a part of the body of Adam. Every soul that comes from each of these 613 parts of the body of Adam is intrinsically connected to every other soul coming from that same part by a common soul root. Depending on what part of the body a soul root comes from determines much of its overall temperament, worldview, and ultimately, its tikkun. For example, a soul root that comes from the brain of Adam will have a very different orientation and purpose in life than one from his heel or hand.

According to the Arizal there are a number of general categories of souls. After Adam sinned, his spiritual stature fell dramatically and was greatly reduced. This fall was accompanied by souls that left his body and entered into the realms of the *klipot*, the impure and unholy "shells," which mired these souls in spiritual contamination. Nonetheless, they still draw their ultimate source back to one of the parts of the body of Adam. Other souls remained in the body of Adam and these souls went into Cain and Abel, who become the archetypal embodiments of the left side of gevurah, the aspect of strict judgment (Cain), and the right side of chessed, "loving-kindness" (Abel). Therefore the Arizal, when discussing the origins of souls, constantly traces their source back to Cain and Abel.

The book of Ecclesiastes, as discussed in Chapter One, opens with these words: "The words of Kohelet, the son of David, king in Jerusalem. 'Vanity of vanities,' says Kohelet, 'vanity of vanities, all is vanity.'" The word for "vanity" is *hevel*, the same as the name of Abel in Hebrew. This is explained in Kabbalah to mean that all vanity in this world is connected to the ongoing cycle of reincarnated souls, who are all connected to Abel, as his death produced the first reincarnation in Seth.

In addition to the souls that came from Adam, the Arizal described a type of soul he termed a "new soul" that does not originate in Adam; rather it is a special soul that comes from the higher world of Atzilut, which exists above the lower three worlds of Beriah, Yetzirah, and Assiyah, all three of which are manifest in creation. The souls contained in Adam come from these three lower worlds. The more unique "new souls" come into the world on rare occasions when there is a great need for new inspiration or leadership. (In a different context, the term, "new soul," is also used to describe a soul during its first time in a body, as discussed above.)

Until this point the teachings of the Arizal have been fairly easy to follow. As he begins to magnify each specific aspect of the soul roots in Adam, though the basic model becomes more complex, similar to the above examples we have shared from the world of science. Each of the Kabbalistic worlds is comprised of five *partzufim* – which in the terminology of the Arizal are specific constellations of sefirot – and each *partzuf* (sing. of *partzufim*) in turn corresponds to the five levels of soul. Each partzuf then divides into 613 parts: 248 organs and 365 sinews. Since each partzuf, which corresponds to a specific level of soul, also includes all five levels of soul as described by the principle of inter-inclusion discussed earlier, each of the five levels will in fact have five x five levels of 613 parts. These twenty-five levels of 613 major soul roots are all in one world. This process repeats itself in the four worlds of Atzilut, Beriah, Yetzirah, and Assiyah.

All of these major soul roots then divide into 613 major soul sparks. Therefore there are 613 x 613 major soul sparks at each of the above-mentioned levels. These major soul sparks also subdivide further into minor soul sparks, but here the number is no longer consistent. Some may subdivide into a hundred minor sparks and some into a thousand. The maximum number of minor sparks coming from a major spark, however, cannot exceed 600,000 (see Kabbalaonline.org, *Gate of Reincarnations*, 11:2–5. Trans. Yitzchok Bar Chaim. Commentary by Shabtai Teicher).

When following this progression we see that there are an extremely large number of possible minor soul sparks that are connected back to a smaller number of major soul sparks. These then connect back to a smaller number of major soul roots that are traced back to the five levels of partzufim in each world, which ultimately are manifest in the soul/body of Adam. The Arizal further explains that each of the 613 organs and sinews at its source are also divided into three levels of "flesh," "tendon," and "bone," from the more external to the more internal. Just as a soul coming from the right eye of Adam is essentially different than a soul coming from the left shoulder, similarly a soul coming from the more external "flesh" would have a different demeanor and direction than a soul coming from the more internal "bone." These various levels within each organ or sinew can, for example, be used to account for the diversity among Jews: from scholars, who relate to the more inner levels, to those who excel more at doing mitzvot, to the more unlearned strata of society, represented by the more external aspect of each part.

This complex system is quite remarkable in its similarity to modern scientific methods of analyzing in greater and greater detail the atom, cell, the DNA double helix, or the workings of the various biological systems in the human body, like the eye or the brain. This scientific process has yielded deep and extensive practical knowledge, more than could ever have been imagined. The Arizal's analysis of how the macro body/soul structure of Adam progresses into the micro-manifestation of individual souls is to be seen in the same way.

The Arizal in a related, but slightly different, organizational model explains how all these soul roots first contained in Adam, who was an all-inclusive soul, were replicated in the Jewish people. In this model, the progression follows the historic development of the Jewish people as recorded in the Torah. All of the soul roots initially included in Adam were made manifest within the three Patriarchs – Abraham, Isaac, and Jacob. Subsequently, the soul roots incorporated in the Patriarchs were included within the twelve sons of Jacob, the progenitors of the twelve tribes of Israel. These twelve then split into the seventy souls that went down to Egypt with Jacob. These seventy souls, or minor roots, were then transformed or reorganized into 600,000 minor sparks.

The number 600,000 is very significant for it is the number of men between the ages of twenty and sixty who came out of Egypt and stood at Mount Sinai. According to Kabbalah these

600,000 souls are also archetypal and represent the totality of Jewish souls throughout the generations. In addition, this figure is the amount of letters in the Torah, as taught in Kabbalah and Chassidut. According to this teaching there exists a clear and essential correlation between the souls of Israel and the letters in the Torah. Similar to how a Torah scroll is invalid if even one of its letters is missing or damaged, so too the Jewish people are considered incomplete if any Jew is lost, estranged, or blemished. This teaching relates beautifully to the major purpose of reincarnation as discussed throughout the book – that God uses reincarnation to insure that no soul is ultimately lost.

The notion that the all-inclusive soul of Adam is reproduced in the Patriarchs and transferred and subdivided through the generations reflects a deep understanding of the words of the sages when they say: "You [Israel] are called Adam and not the other nations of the world" (*Yevamot* 61a). In light of these teachings of reincarnation we can understand this to mean that although all souls are ultimately included in the soul of Adam in a particular way, the all-inclusive nature of the soul of Adam is manifest exclusively in the Jewish people.

Although what we have presented in this section on soul roots may seem complicated, in all truth it pales in comparison to a full immersion in the vast sea of details regarding the dynamics of reincarnation in general, and of soul roots and sparks in particular. As we have pointed out, these specifics are being presented here not for the sake of detail; rather, they reveal a deep and profound understanding of the complexity of the soul and of life itself. Yet it is very important not to get bogged down in the details of the Arizal's system at the expense of extracting the inner dimension of meaning from the various models presented in this chapter. Therefore, we will now attempt to formulate the important implications of soul roots and sparks from what we have learned above, as well as additional teachings from the Arizal relating to the subject.

Perhaps the prime thought to emerge from understanding soul roots is how individual soul sparks are connected to ever larger constellations of minor and major soul roots, all connected to a specific part of the body/soul of Adam. For many in the Western world in particular this idea may seem not only strange, but it runs against the strong emphasis on independence and autonomy engrained within its various societies. The idea of each person as king or queen of their own castle, coupled with the capitalistic ethos of acquiring more and more material wealth, has created a worldview in which the individual reigns supreme. This attitude is not entirely negative. When applied properly it gives individuals a high degree of motivation to develop themselves to their fullest potential and establishes important guidelines protecting an individual's freedoms and rights. Unfortunately, given the limits of human nature, this overemphasis on the individual has led modern societies to be ruled by unbridled egotism, selfishness, and exaggerated self-reliance, producing a relatively shallow culture of instant gratification, an unending bombardment of stimuli, and a "dog eat dog" world.

A Jewish worldview also emphasizes the sanctity of the individual, as found in sayings such as, "Whoever saves one life, it is as if he has saved an entire world" and "Therefore every individual is obligated to say, 'For my sake was the world created" (*Mishnah, Sanhedrin* 4:5). Yet this awareness of the importance of the individual is always tempered with the knowledge that an individual Jew is also part of a much bigger reality. Every Jew is reminded in countless ways of being a link in an eternal chain of a people steeped in communal tradition and history, of being part of a nation whose fate and destiny connects all the individual parts into a much greater whole. Perhaps the teaching that most encapsulates the balance between the individual and the collective is found in the saying of Hillel: "If I am not for myself – who will be? And if I am only for myself – what am I?" (*Pirkei Avot* 1:14). In essence, the teachings of the Arizal regarding soul roots are simply an exposition on how that greater whole actually works.

Kabbalah teaches that although there are 600,000 archetypal Jewish souls, they are in essence all bound together in one essential unified whole. That is the importance of what the Arizal meant when he said that the Patriarchs were also all-inclusive souls, just like Adam. This is the reason we begin the essential prayer of Judaism, the silent *Amida*, with the words: "Blessed are You, God, the God of Abraham, the God of Isaac, and the God of Jacob." In other rituals and prayers as well we make mention of the Patriarchs and Matriarchs in order to remind ourselves of our common heritage, and even deeper, of our common soul root.

In the Arizal's system of thought, souls that originate in a common soul spark or root share a common fate and interest. If one soul achieves tikkun in some way it elevates all the other souls of that spark or root; conversely, if one soul is blemished it negatively affects all the other component pieces. This provides profound insight into the statement, "All of Israel is responsible one for the other." Therefore, all the souls of a certain root in a sense "cheer" each other on and assist each other through ibbur and gilgul. When a soul enters this world in ibbur it does so with a soul of a similar root or spark, and when a number of souls reincarnate in one body they also will each be of the same spark or root. These teachings broaden what "extended family" means.

This description of soul roots certainly offers us a very different paradigm for knowing who and what an individual is. There is no doubt that to be able to properly integrate this concept into one's mind-set would take much thought. One should not think that this paradigm is in any way a recipe for a lack of individuality or for being lost in a faceless collective soul conglomeration. If anything it increases a sense of uniqueness in that it emphasizes an elevated feeling of distinctive responsibility to develop ourselves to our fullest potential and accomplish what only we can do. It is as if the whole world is dependent on our every action; Maimonides taught that one should see the world at every moment as perfectly balanced between good and evil, and that my next action has the power to tip the scales (*Mishneh Torah, Hilchot Teshuva* 3:4). This then is the ultimate description of the uniqueness of the individual.

As a consequence of the false feeling of individuality based on ego and selfishness so prevalent in the world today there is an almost desperate desire by so many to belong to something greater than one's own narrow and limited concept of self. Despite stimuli and gadgets galore that provide instant gratification, it seems people are lonelier and more isolated than ever. The Arizal explains that though we may be unaware of it, in essence we are not alone; we all belong to something greater than ourselves. Jews have managed to survive as a people in no small measure due to a core belief that as important as the individual is, there is a greater communal good to which we are subservient, a grander destiny that links us together.

MORE ON IBBUR

We continue here the discussion we began earlier regarding the concept of ibbur, "impregnation." Although gilgul is considered a higher level of tikkun than ibbur, there are many ways in which ibbur is an even greater chessed from God. First, ibbur is one of the ways that God helps those who are sincerely interested in change and improvement. Receiving assistance from the soul of a tzaddik in order to accomplish what one could not do on his or her own is certainly a great chessed, for instead of having to wait until returning in another lifetime, the assistance provided by ibbur allows one to elevate his or her self in a current lifetime.

Another chessed inherent in ibbur is that sometimes a departed soul needs just a small repair which can be accomplished by attaching itself to a soul in this world for a short time and sharing in the performance of a mitzvah or good deed. Although the host soul is not consciously aware of this, he earns great merit through his chessed to the departed soul who has so returned. We have seen consistently that the principles and dynamics of reincarnation are part of a larger context of mainstream Jewish ideas. There is a basic belief in Judaism that doing good deeds, giving charity, learning Torah, and the like, in the name of a departed soul assists it in its immediate period of rectification and even long after. This is particularly true of saying kaddish, the mourner's prayer, and commemorating the *yahrtzeit,* the yearly anniversary of a person's passing. Here too, with ibbur we may be assisting departed souls in their quest for tikkun and elevation. The difference is in the case of ibbur we are not aware of what we are doing, whereas when we say kaddish we are very conscious of our connection with a departed soul and the merit our acts create for it.

Although a person is not consciously aware of ibbur it is clear that many times we feel a "presence" or new vitality, inspiration, or strength to break through a formidable obstacle in our lives. Often after years of trying to change certain attitudes or personality traits, a breakthrough occurs suddenly and almost unexpectedly. This may be attributed to an incidence of ibbur.

As previously explained, if a person does not achieve a full tikkun during his first incarnation, the period most favorable for achieving full rectification, he or she can then accomplish this goal only one soul level at a time, necessitating one to pass away and return again to receive the next level of soul. The Arizal notes that ibbur is an exception to this and that with ibbur one can go from level to level in the same lifetime. This is yet another advantage ibbur holds over needing a full lifetime in another gilgul.

Through ibbur, the impregnated soul only stands to gain and not to lose. Thus, says the Arizal, the impregnated soul does not share in the pain or the sins of the host soul. Indeed, if the host soul consistently sins the ibbur will leave. If, on the other hand, the pain can somehow help the departed soul further its spiritual needs, then it does feel the pain, but it still does not share in the responsibility of sin.

There are three types of souls discussed in Jewish tradition:

tzaddikim, "righteous ones," *benonim*, "intermediary souls," and *resha'im*, "evildoers." There are many different opinions as to what constitutes each of these categories. Rabbi Shneur Zalman of Liady begins his classic work, *Tanya*, with a discussion of these three divisions. In his opinion the level of tzaddik is for all intents and purposes beyond the grasp of virtually everyone and that just being a *benoni* (sing. of *benonim*) takes a lifetime of effort. (Other opinions would consider the Tanya's description of a benoni to be a tzaddik.) Although the entire *Tanya* follows this basic tone he does say that one of the ways to reach the level of tzaddik is to be assisted by the ibbur of the soul of a tzaddik. This is consistent with the teaching of the Arizal that in the coming world a soul that receives an ibbur, and through this assistance accomplishes great things, does not have his reward either decreased as a result or split with the assisting soul. The soul earns a full reward as if it accomplished those great things on its own.

In the same way that there exist in the world forces of positive and negative attraction, so too in the spiritual realms. The Arizal taught that when a person does a mitzvah in total sincerity and for the sake of heaven it has an immense effect and, above in the higher worlds, it stirs the souls of the tzaddikim that come from the same soul root. Since all souls from the same root are intrinsically connected and assist each other in achieving tikkun, the power of this mitzvah may draw one of these souls down in ibbur, and then through the combined efforts of these souls great spiritual results can be effected. That is the secret meaning of "two are better than one" (Ecclesiastes 4:9). In the same fashion, our understanding of ibbur and gilgul reveal an even deeper appreciation of the statement in *Pirkei Avot* (4:2): "...for one mitzvah leads to another mitzvah, and one sin leads to another sin; for the consequence [reward] of a mitzvah is [another] mitzvah and the consequence of a sin is [another] sin." Just as we have seen the effects of positive energy as relates to souls of the same soul spark or root, so too negative energy created by un-rectified thoughts, speech, and action in this world has a ripple effect on souls in the upper worlds.

Rabbi Yitzchak Ginsburgh reveals many deep connections between ibbur and gilgul based on their numerical values. The word ibbur, when in its full or 'plene' spelling (i.e., with the letter *yud*), has a numerical value of 288, and its letters can be rearranged to spell *ya'avor*, meaning "he will cross [over]." Ibbur represents a soul "crossing over" from the world of souls to this material world.

The number 288 is an extremely important number in Kabbalah, as it is the symbolic number of how many principal sparks fell below in the "breaking of the vessels," the catastrophic cosmological event that, according to the Arizal, occurred when the initial immature vessels of creation shattered from the intensity of the primordial light. The 288 sparks of holiness from the original light became trapped in the fallen vessels and it is our mission to redeem and elevate those sparks. The numerical value of ibbur equaling 288 alludes to the very purpose of ibbur and gilgul as well – to redeem and uplift all the sparks of the soul until it achieves its full tikkun.

Rabbi Ginsburgh continues his numerical analysis by directing attention to the fact that ibbur (288) is four times the value of gilgul (72). A ratio of 1:4 is an exceptionally important one in Kabbalah and can be seen three times in the Torah account of the creation of Adam, the first human, and the Garden of Eden:

> "These are the generations of the heaven and the earth when they were created, in the day that Hashem God made earth and heaven. And all the plants of the field were not yet on the earth and all the herbs of the field had not yet sprouted, for Hashem God had not caused it to rain upon the earth and there was no man to work the ground. A mist ascended from the earth and watered the whole surface of the ground. And Hashem God

formed the man of dust from the ground, and He blew into his nostrils the soul of life; and man became a living being. Hashem God planted a garden in Eden, to the east, and placed there the man whom He had formed. And Hashem God caused to sprout from the ground every tree that was pleasing to the sight and good for food; and the Tree of Life in the midst of the garden, and the Tree of Knowledge of Good and Evil. A river issues forth from Eden to water the garden, and from there it is divided and becomes four headwaters" (Genesis 2: 4–10).

The first time we see the 1:4 relationship is in the letters of the Hebrew word for "mist," *ed*, that rose from the earth. The letters of this word are *alef* and *dalet* and are respectively valued at 1 and 4. Next we find the ratio of 1:4 in the two named trees of the garden, the Tree of Knowledge of Good and Evil and the Tree of Life, where the value of the former (932) is four times the value of the latter (233). Finally we see that the river flowing out of the Garden divided into four streams.

The ultimate example, though, of the 1:4 ratio is that of One God who is revealed in the world through the Tetragrammaton, the four-letter name. Rabbi Ginsburgh explains that this same 1:4 ratio is the secret of modern science's quest for the unified field theory which hopes to unite in one equation the four principle forces of the physical world as described by modern science: gravity, electromagnetism, the strong nuclear force, and the weak nuclear force. In fact, much of the physical world emanating from God's essential oneness is described in terms of sets of four, such as the four elements: fire, air, water and earth; solid, liquid, gas and combustion; the four seasons, the four directions, and the description of creation being categorized by man, animal, vegetable, and mineral.

In regard to gilgul and ibbur, this same ratio informs us that at times a soul can accomplish in one ibbur what would have taken four gilgulim. This is an additional chessed contained in ibbur. Even deeper is the realization that both ibbur and gilgul occur for the sake of redeeming the 288 fallen sparks of creation, each soul playing its unique part in the redemption of the world. The four rivers flowing out of one primary river in Eden symbolizes how we need to look beyond the apparent multiplicity and dualities of this world with the aim of seeing the essential oneness of God permeating every point of time and space. Finally, the mist that rose up to water the face of the earth represents what is termed "the arousal from below," just like doing a mitzvah with such deep spiritual intent awakens heavenly assistance to flow.

Although the concept of ibbur may be new to most people, and at first may seem somewhat strange and even "spooky," when understood properly it yields a deep understanding of our own psyche and can explain many things that would otherwise remain a mystery. There is no doubt that truly integrating these teachings demands a fundamental paradigm shift in the way we look at ourselves and others, as well as our most basic perceptions regarding reality and the meaning and dynamics of life. Yet just as modern science has not only revealed but proven in the laboratory the verity of a radical and revolutionary description of the world in which we live that truly stretches the imagination beyond all previous limits, so too the Jewish teachings of ibbur and gilgul reveal a deeper look at reality and a more profound appreciation for what "makes us tick."

WOMEN AND REINCARNATION

One of the topics concerning which there exists some uncertainty regarding the Arizal's true teachings on the subject is the theme of women and reincarnation. This is not the only topic in which subsequent generations struggled to understand his thought. Questions about his position on various matters are bound to arise for two reasons we have already pointed out: he did not record his own writings and he only taught for a relatively short period of time (recall that he died at the age of 38). Therefore our current issue of women and reincarnation must be approached bearing this in mind.

In the *Gate of Reincarnations* (9) it states clearly that gilgul applies to men and not to women. The verse, "A generation goes and a generation comes but the earth stands forever" (Ecclesiastes 1:4), is interpreted as "a generation goes and a generation comes" through gilgul and refers specifically to men, whereas "the earth," represents the feminine energy (mother earth), "stands forever," thus indicating that women do not go through gilgul. This view is supported by the emphasis placed on the words, "with a man," in the verse from Job: "Thus God does all these things twice or three times *with a man*, to bring back his soul from the pit, to be enlightened with the light of the living."

A second explanation is offered; since men fulfill the mitzvah to study Torah, they are protected from having to enter gehenom, however, in order to cleanse themselves of the blemish of whatever sins they have committed, they must reincarnate. Given that women generally do not study Torah to the degree men do, they rectify their sins through the experience of gehenom. It should be noted again, as was explained at the beginning of this chapter, the idea that men who study Torah are immune from gehenom is itself a very relative concept and hardly applies to all men.

Before we go further it needs to be stated that the above remarks concerning who goes through gilgul and who goes through gehenom are not necessarily value judgments as much as a question of the dynamics of how a soul achieves its tikkun. Although gilgul occurs within the overriding context of God's chessed, there is no doubt that it implies a judgment based on a person's need for tikkun. Gehenom too, in a sense, aims at accomplishing the same goal, only in a shorter and more intense manner. Although gilgul would appear to be a more appealing option, it is not clear that returning to this earth so many times, with all the challenges, pain, and suffering that this frequently entails, is a "better" option than a shorter "crash course" in soul rectification. On the other hand, there are certain advantages inherent in the opportunity to return and study Torah and do mitzvot.

In any event, the rectified parts of the soul of both men and women need no further tikkun, each receiving their reward in the next world and the promise of the ultimate reward in the World to Come. It is only a matter of how the un-rectified parts of the soul reach their tikkun.

If that would be all that the Arizal transmitted about our present issue, his position would be clear. But that is not all he taught. In the same section referred to above he continues by saying that women do come in ibbur, especially to assist other women who cannot conceive due to their having a female body but a male soul. In such a case, a woman who comes in ibbur can help this woman give birth, and frequently reincarnate into the newborn child. In our discussion of ibbur we saw how, in certain respects, it is an even higher expression of God's chessed than gilgul.

In the twentieth section of the *Gate of Reincarnations*, and in the thirteenth section of *Sefer Hagilgulim*, a complementary book of teachings of the Arizal edited by Rabbi Meir Popperos (1624–1662), the Arizal states that women do reincarnate along with their soul mates, as they are essentially connected, being two halves of one whole. Thus, if one of those parts is in need of rectification, it would naturally follow that the other half also be in need of rectification, or at least needs to participate in the tikkun. Based on this it can be assumed that if men reincarnate on an ongoing basis, women do as well. In fact, in the commentary *Bnei Aharon*, on the initial statement by the Arizal in the ninth section of the *Gate of Reincarnations* quoted above stating that women do not reincarnate, he immediately writes that one should refer to the other statements by the Arizal that woman do, in fact, reincarnate along with their husbands.

Gilgulei Neshamot, a book mentioned earlier in Chapter One, is an alphabetized summary of the teachings of the Arizal on the entire spectrum of the subject compiled from the full range of his teachings. A good amount of the soul histories contained therein relate to women and their reincarnations. In many cases the women's reincarnations are connected to their husbands', while in others they are recounted independently of their husbands'.

When taking these two views of the Arizal together – the original statement which seemed to categorically exclude women from gilgul, along with his other teachings which recognize gilgul for women, especially in the case of soul mates, we can now appreciate more fully the uncertainty mentioned at the start of this section.

One thing that can be theorized, and this is based on the second reason why women do not go through reincarnation – that they do not study Torah; men, as will be recalled, are immune from gehenom in the merit of their Torah study, is that the world has changed dramatically since the time of the Arizal in regard to women and the study of Torah. In earlier generations, women did not receive a formal education but were instead home-trained and whatever Torah they did learn was usually in conjunction with those areas particularly relevant and practical to their family life. Today, it is taken for granted that women in the Jewish religious world will receive a formal education that includes the study of Torah. Indeed, many women study in conjunction with their raising families and having careers. The question that can at least be asked is, would the Arizal understand or even receive from Heaven a different understanding based on this new reality? Or on a deeper level, it could be pondered whether the increased participation of women in Torah learning has actually changed their reality in respect to gilgul.

In light of the above we now present a number of insights from Rabbi Ginsburgh, a leading authority on Kabbalistic matters. In his opinion the many exceptions noted by the Arizal in fact become the rule, and so for all practical purposes, when studying the subject of gilgul today we understand it as applying to both men and women. We do not in any way discount anything that the Arizal taught, but we do interpret it within the wider scope of his teachings.

In Rabbi Ginsburgh's view, not only do women reincarnate, in a sense they "direct" and "turn" the revolving wheel of gilgul. He derives this from the fact that it was Eve who first caused death by eating of the Tree of Knowledge of Good and Evil. Paradoxically, Eve who caused death is named Chava, "And the man called his wife Chava," which comes from the root that means life, "because she was the mother of all living" (Genesis 3:20). The paradox of the one who brought death into the world being called the "mother of all living" reminds us of the central verse the Arizal used to explain the dynamics of reincarnation: "Thus God does all these things twice or three times with a man, to bring back his soul from the pit, *to be enlightened with the light of the living*." The rectification of death is to be "enlightened with the light of the living," the primary goal of reincarnation.

Another verse that points to women "directing" reincarnation is (Jeremiah 31:21) "…God has created a new thing in the earth – a woman courts a man." This verse alludes to the Messianic future when women will assume an equal status with men, a phenomenon known as *tikkun Chava*, "the rectification of Eve." The word in the verse for "courts" is more literally defined as "surrounds." Rabbi Ginsburgh teaches that not only does a woman surround a man, as reminiscent of a bride circling her groom under the Jewish wedding canopy, but even more so, it is the woman who is in fact "turning" the man. The word "surrounds," in this verse is similar in meaning to gilgul, in that they both have to do with turning, and alludes to revealing the role of women in "directing" the dynamic of reincarnation. He further cites the verse, "A generation goes and a generation comes but the earth stands forever" (Ecclesiastes 1:4), as an allusion to the woman symbolizing the earth around which the generations, as it were, rotate in gilgul. This is consistent with the Kabbalistic teaching that the power that moves everything else, itself does not move.

Rabbi Ginsburgh adds to these ideas the references in the

Zohar to the *Shechina*, the feminine aspect of the Divine, as being related to the galgal hayareach, the cycle of the moon. Women throughout Jewish tradition have been associated with the moon, a feminine symbol, in contrast to the sun, a masculine symbol.

Time is intrinsically associated with women, especially through her monthly biorhythm and the connection of the Jewish calendar to the moon's cycles. What makes the Jewish calendar unique is that along with being based on a lunar cycle, it also stays aligned to the solar year through a nineteen-year cycle in which there are seven leap years. These leap years, called "pregnant years," are formed by adding an extra month at the end of the year. The numerical value of Chava is also nineteen, alluding to the connection between the first woman and the nineteen-year cycle of time on which the Jewish calendar is founded. The number seven, the amount of leap years in the nineteen-year cycle is also a feminine concept, as Shabbat, the seventh day, is symbolized as a bride, the epitome of feminine energy.

Another beautiful allusion in interpreting the verse as "a woman surrounds a man," is found in its numerical equivalent of 832, being the same as *Eretz Yisrael*, "the Land of Israel." The physical Land of Israel, as tiny as it may appear, is strategically situated in the middle of the world at the crossroads of Europe, Asia, and Africa. Because of this, every empire since the time of Abraham has sought to control it. Not only has Israel played a central role in politics, economics, religion, and all facets of human development, it has actually directed the revolving dynamics of history around her.

The reference to Israel as "her" is midrashically related to viewing the Land of Israel as a bride for the people of Israel, the groom. This metaphor is seen clearly throughout the Song of Songs where the man in the parable representing God is constantly describing his beloved, the people of Israel, in images of the Land of Israel. Here we see that in relation to God the Jewish people are like a bride, whereas in relation to the Land of Israel, the Jewish people are like the groom.

Rabbi Ginsburgh further states that whereas men reincarnate in order to rectify Adam, women reincarnate in order to rectify Eve. For this reason the Arizal taught that the Patriarchs were all involved in rectifying the sin of Adam, while the Matriarchs were all involved in fixing the sin of Eve.

PEOPLE IN OUR LIVES

Now that we have explained some of the many general and specific dynamics of reincarnation, we turn to contemplate how these ideas become manifest in our lives. From all that we have learned, one should conclude that the people we encounter in our lives are not a random collection of coincidental meetings, but are connected to us in the deepest way. Considering how many people leave this world with unfinished business and unresolved relationships, it is not surprising that the teachings on reincarnation alert us to the fact that much of what happens in our current lives is meant to tie up loose ends. If one has strong feelings about some aspect of himself being left over from a previous lifetime, he or she should trust their emotions and seek out a proper course of action to heal those open wounds. While there can be no certainty in this regard, Rabbi Ginsburgh teaches people to trust their instincts. And what is true concerning one's self-impressions is also true about his impressions of the relationships he has with others.

Not only are people connected by a web of relationships weaving through the generations, but as can be imagined, these can sometimes be manifest in peculiar ways as well. For example, in one lifetime two souls may be paired as parent-child, teacher-student, pursuer-pursued, or loaner-borrower, while in another the roles may be reversed, or may repeat over and over again, each time matching the soul with the condition that will most aid it in its ultimate goal. A group of friends, siblings, or students of a particular teacher may at times return in similar groupings, and soul mates may return many times together until accomplishing their individual and joint tasks in life.

These deep soul connections can often be seen in the relationship of rabbi, sage, or rebbe with his students and followers. It would often happen that a student would come to one Chassidic rebbe only to be sent to another when the first perceived that the student was not of his soul root, but was more attached to the soul root of the second. One can also see these connections in a person whose outward behavior leaves much to be desired and yet he is still drawn to a tzaddik. This is because both good and evil can come from the same root soul. In these cases the tzaddik will labor tirelessly to bring the less desirable soul back to the good, as all souls of a similar root or spark are intimately bound together.

Sometimes a very righteous person will have children who turn to the paths of evil. Since each person has so many different levels of tikkun to undergo, those un-rectified traits may emerge, like a previously dormant gene, to become a dominant character trait in one of his or her progeny. This can also work in the opposite manner when a grossly unrefined person gives birth to a very high soul. The person in this case is not totally evil and his latent good nature, which may be hidden, only comes to the fore in his descendants. This can help us understand the family dynamics of many a biblical figure, especially in the case of the Patriarchs and Matriarchs, who number Ishmael and Esau among their kin. In these instances of biblical siblings the individuals involved developed in very different ways. On a whole, this can be explained as being part of the process of "clarifying good from bad" in those individuals, as well as in the parents who sired them.

For example, Jacob's archetypal battle with a mysterious being before confronting his brother Esau occurred on many levels simultaneously. On one level Jacob was trying to clarify the side of himself that was still figuratively holding on to the heel of Esau. Not only did Jacob need to confront evil in the external form of Esau, but equally important was his need to purge himself of his own internal character blemishes. As a result of a lifetime of spiritual work Jacob fathered twelve sons, all of whom were righteous.

Now one may ask about the tribes: how righteous could they have been to have sold their own brother into slavery? In response, one should realize that the sale of Joseph is a far more complicated subject than what is revealed by a cursory reading of the biblical text and is full of profound matters pertaining to Divine Providence and free will. Especially in light of all that we have said thus far, we can see that much of what is truly transpiring between people is quite hidden from our conscious minds and hearts. And in Joseph's own words: "And now do not be distressed or reproach yourselves for having sold me here, for it was to be a provider that God sent me before you" (Genesis 45:5).

According to the Arizal, a person can do something very wrong and still be on a high soul level. Certainly he will have to take responsibility and rectify the deed in this life or in another, but it does not mean the soul loses all its previous levels of accomplishment. And of course, only God knows what the true accounting of a life is, let alone the full story of each individual throughout history. A good example is King David whose actions with Bat Sheva left much to be desired. For his misdeeds he actively repented the rest of his life, and although it was considered a grievous blemish on his soul, he never lost his connection to God or forfeited his spiritual accomplishments.

Returning to the subject of understanding the various strata of the relationships in our lives, the Arizal stated that various components of one soul may be spread out among a number of people, these being the people in one's life, with each one trying to elevate a particular aspect of the common soul. These can be friends striving together for their mutual benefit, or alternatively, one may draw all the positive aspects of his own soul from the other person, while the other draws all the negative aspects from the first. The phenomenon of seeing glimpses of ourselves or others close to us manifest in other people takes on a startling reality according to this perspective.

And if friends or students of one rabbi may return in pairs or groups to continue growing together, so too enemies or competitors may return to do battle again. This, as we saw above, is the secret of the souls of Cain and Abel returning generation after generation, endlessly struggling with each other until their archetypal conflict is once and for all resolved.

These complicated relationships bridging various lifetimes explain much of what we refer to as the "chemistry" between people. We all know that instinctively we are drawn to or repulsed by others. Sometimes we may intuit the reason, but many times it transcends our comprehension.

At times, these attractions are very powerful and lead to wonderful things; and at other times, they lead to the pit of destruction. Based on our presentation, these interactions can be fathomed in the light of gilgul and as consequences of past actions.

At the very least, our relationships in this lifetime should alert us to the tremendous opportunity we have to rectify, clarify, and forge ahead in fulfilling our mission in life. The people and circumstances around us are there for a reason. As the Slonimer Rebbe said, "If you want to know what you need to fix in this world, look at those areas that are the hardest for you." This applies equally to relationships. Some of us react to these situations by avoiding those with whom we have difficulties, yet it is fascinating to consider how when we repair these strained relations we are simultaneously elevating ourselves. And we certainly climb to new soul heights when cultivating the positive relationships in our lives, drawing ever closer to the soul's consummate refinement.

It is less important to know who you were in a previous lifetime than to know that each life is an opportunity to rectify the soul in the most fundamental way. Our focus should be on the present; nevertheless, knowing that the present is shaped by the past gives us insight into those areas we need most to repair. With a keen eye to seeing beyond the present, we are given ongoing prospects in this life to not only finish old business, but to forge new paths to fulfilling our purpose in life.

THE MATRIX

When all the ramifications and implications of the teachings on reincarnation from a Jewish view are properly understood, they present a far different reality than meets the eye. Similar to how modern science explains the true nature of the physical universe in terms that boggle the imagination, especially as it seems to fly in the face of our normative experience of the world, so too the teachings on reincarnation present a picture of reality far different from the one we are accustomed to and take for granted.

Both modern science and Kabbalah posit that in essence all time exists simultaneously and is not linear as our senses seem to tell us. We mentioned above that the numeric value of gilgul equals 72, the same as the sum of the words *haya*, "past," *hoveh*, "present," and *veyihiyeh*, "and future." Science describes the simultaneous aspect of time being achieved at the speed of light, while we all experience daily how our consciousness flows fluidly between the present moment and thoughts of the past and dreams of the future.

The realization of all time being ever-present expands our notion of time to envision it as a matrix, a fluid cross-dimensional medium encompassing all that ever happened or ever will. This idea is not as far-fetched as it may sound. Today in the physical world we have a similar matrix formed by the global communications network, especially the World Wide Web. A combination of satellites, fiber optics, wires, cables, and chips connect the world in such a manner that through telephone, electronic mail, fax, television, radio, and Internet connections, we are receivers and transmitters of instantaneous communication with every corner of the globe. In the physical world, this matrix extends only through the present, but in the non-physical, spiritual reality, all time converges. It is through the understanding of the teachings on gilgul that we come to realize that souls too are connected together through past, present, and future.

We have seen through the teachings of soul roots, soul mates, and the different levels of soul that manifest in an incredible web of relationships, how interconnected souls are in one lifetime and through the generations. Even more so, understanding gilgul allows us to break through the barrier between the material and spiritual worlds. Ultimately, the matrix of time and souls transcends our normative conceptions of the division between life and death itself.

This is not only a mystical view of things, but is the simple understanding inherent in the many Jewish laws and customs relating to the mourning process, as discussed earlier. We accept the notion that by reciting kaddish, learning Torah, reciting psalms, or giving charity in the name of a deceased person, we are adding merit to them and assisting their souls, especially during the first year after death when the soul undergoes an intense period of tikkun and purification. We assume even without the belief in gilgul that souls remain connected to the living even after death.

The *Sefer Yetzirah*, one of the earliest Kabbalistic texts, speaks of reality being a unification of the dimensions of *olam*, "world" or space, *shana*, "year" or time, and *nefesh*, "soul." It was only a hundred years ago that Einstein connected the dimensions of time and space. Since then, science, especially quantum physics, has begun to recognize consciousness (soul) as an intrinsic ingredient of reality as well. We have thus in this section described three different aspects of the matrix of reality: the unity of past, present, and future in regard to time, the web of communications in regard to space, and gilgul linking souls in the present and throughout the generations.

The matrix of time, space, and soul exists, but unless we choose to acknowledge this truth it will remain beyond our everyday experience. Entering into the matrix necessitates not only a conscious choice but grace from Above, as recognizing this requires a higher and more expanded consciousness than most people are capable of achieving through their efforts alone. Yet we all get glimpses of it, whether through meditation, prayer, intellectual probing, Torah study, dreams, or understanding Divine Providence as it plays itself out in our lives.

If nothing else, the teachings of gilgul we have discussed leave us with the feeling that life is so much more complex, deep, and profound than we imagine. The invisible web of space, time, and soul draws every aspect of reality together in order that we should be aware of the unity of all things. This unity is the manifestation of the oneness of God, the essence of all reality.

CHAPTER FIVE:

Reincarnation and History

The common expression, "history repeats itself," informs us by its very widespread usage that just like there are cycles in nature – the seasons, the waxing and waning of the moon, etc. – so too are there historical cycles and repeating patterns. Although history, like time, would appear to pass in a strictly linear fashion from past to future, in a more profound view it can be seen to unfold in a circular fashion, or even more precisely, as an upward spiral. Due to the nature of the Torah's calendar, which follows the cycles of the week and Shabbat, the repeating rhythm of the moon, and the yearly reoccurrence of holidays, Jewish thought and lifestyle are finely attuned to the above perspective. Jewish history has especially brought this theme home for us through its ongoing cycle of exile and redemption and then exile again on a grander, national level, and in countless villages, cities, kingdoms, countries, and empires throughout the Diaspora on a smaller scale.

As discussed earlier, Jewish belief is based on the idea of a creation infused with Divine purpose and direction, whether relating to the individual, the Jewish people, or humanity as a whole. Therefore, in a Torah view, history is the record of man's development and striving towards the ultimate Divine goal. Secular thought, which does not posit any overarching meaning, direction, or Providence to history, or to creation for that matter, runs against the grain of all Jewish thought.

Not only does the Torah suggest a directed purpose to creation, all history according to the oral tradition is driven towards a preprogrammed goal – the Messianic era and the World to Come. The "how" and "when" of getting there are not "written in stone" and are the subject of fascinating debate, but the verity of these coming to pass is something that has been revealed to all the prophets. Just as was discussed with Divine Providence and free will, we see that while the parameters of history are determined, each person's contribution and input is open to the fluctuations of personal choice.

A beautiful connection between time, history, and reincarnation is apparent in the numeric sum of the three words haya, hoveh, veyihiyeh, "past, present, and future," equaling seventy-two, the same numerical value as gilgul, as well as in their sharing the letters of God's four-letter ineffable Name. This hints to time being, along with space, the medium through which God reveals Himself in creation. History, as the record of mankind within the Divinely directed spiral of time, has its repeating cycles and "incarnations" through the generations.

Rabbi Menachem Mendel Schneersohn taught that all of history is a process by which the gola, "exile," rectifies itself and "incarnates" or transforms itself into geula, "redemption." The only difference between these two Hebrew words is that geula has the letter alef within it. The alef symbolizes Godliness in that it is the first letter of the alphabet and many of the names of God begin with this letter. At the time of the final redemption God will reveal not only His true essence to humanity, but how all history enclothed His plan for creation.

The manner in which God is enclothed in history is particularly evident in the story behind the holiday of Purim, which celebrates the successful thwarting of the evil plans of Haman to annihilate all the Jews of Persia, and is recorded in the Scroll of Esther. The commentaries point out that the name of God does not appear even one time in this book. This stresses how oftentimes God acts in a hidden, even mysterious, manner within history in general, and within the specific political and social movements and intrigues of every era. According to tradition there are a number of places in the Scroll of Esther where God's name does in fact appear in acronyms, concealed within the text, and thus highlighting the hidden ways in which God operates in the world. In a remarkable twist, it has been noted that the Hebrew title for this book, *Megilat Esther*, bears striking resemblance to the Hebrew words which mean "revealing the hidden."

According to the Talmud, the present cycle of history is programmed to last six thousand years, culminating in the seventh millennium of the Messianic era (*Sanhedrin* 97a; *Avodah Zarah* 9a; *Rosh Hashanah* 31a). This cycle is intrinsically connected to the primordial pattern of Creation when God created the world in six days and rested on the seventh. The sages state that the letter alef, which also means "a thousand," appears in the first verse of the Torah exactly six times, alluding to the six thousand years of this cycle of creation. The seventh millennium is alluded to in the alef which transforms gola into geula.

The Talmud further divides these six thousand years into three distinct periods – two thousand years of tohu, "confusion," two thousand years of Torah, and two thousand years of the Mashiach, as discussed above. This symbolizes the progression of the world from a state of chaos to the Messianic era, via the channels of Torah. Once again we see God's providential direction acting within the cycles of time and history as humankind exerts its free choice upon the backdrop of the Divine plan of ultimate redemption.

THE DEEDS OF THE FATHERS AND MOTHERS

A phrase often repeated in classic Jewish literature is "The deeds of the fathers are a sign to their children" (*Sota* 34a). This can be understood on many levels. On the simple, most straightforward level, it means the deeds of the Patriarchs and Matriarchs as recorded in the Torah are an ongoing source of moral and ethical lessons for their offspring in all future generations. We read the "stories" of the Torah and are inspired by their lives and their example.

On a deeper level, this phrase intimates that the deeds of the fathers and mothers actually paved the way for their children. Being that the Patriarchs and Matriarchs, along with all the other characters in the Torah, are archetypal figures, their every thought, speech, and action shaped the outer reality, as well as the inner make-up, of all their progeny. We see in the narratives of the Torah archetypal incidents that repeat themselves on multiple levels of existence in every generation. This is especially true in regard to the reoccurrence of events throughout history. This is in fact one of the most fundamental ways in which to understand the Torah, as taught in Kabbalah and Chassidut.

We discussed earlier how Adam was an all-inclusive soul and how in many ways, so too were the Patriarchs and Matriarchs. The power of their deeds lies in their encompassing every future Jewish soul within themselves. In this sense they are Israel's common soul root. We are further taught that all the years Abraham and Sarah did not produce physical children, their thoughts during intimate relations gave birth to, in a spiritual sense, the souls of all future converts. This is one reason why all converts are called the children of Abraham and Sarah. Every action and thought from their lives impressed their energy into the spiritual DNA of every future Jewish soul. We see this same influence, albeit on a somewhat reduced plane, with a parent and a child – the former greatly affecting the latter both through nature and nurture; imprinting their offspring's psychological, emotional, and intellectual states of being through their genetic contribution and through the way they raise their children.

On an even deeper level, the Torah's narratives are not about other people who lived long ago, they are about each and every one of us in every generation; it is our story. This is because we were a part of them and, in certain ways, they are present in us. This is one of the most profound implications of understanding gilgul as it manifests itself in history and in the development of humankind. The phrase quoted above – "All of Israel is responsible (lit., mixed) one for (or with) the other" – certainly applies here when understanding how the souls of the Jewish people are intimately and essentially bound together throughout history, literally mixed together.

In another parallel, we note the development of a human fetus as it appears to progress in its formation through a variety of animal-like stages before assuming a recognizable human shape. So too the soul lives through many eras of history, each one impressing its lessons and spiritual imprint upon it. During the Passover Seder, when we retell the story of how we came out of slavery in Egypt, we recite the following words in the Haggadah: "A person is obligated to see himself as if he came out of Egypt." On a basic level this is teaching us not just to recite the words of the Haggadah, but to attempt to truly relive and experience the story as if it was our own. Kabbalah and Chassidut teach that in truth it is not "as if" we came out of Egypt – our souls actually did, and so the story is really about us! Tradition also teaches that every Jewish soul and every future convert who would ever be born stood together at Mount Sinai when receiving the Torah, just fifty days after leaving Egypt. These teachings are most understandable in the context of gilgul.

Rabbi Avraham Sutton describes beautifully in his book, *The Well of Living Waters* (Jerusalem, 2006. p. 50), how history can be compared to a body. He begins his comparison by citing the teaching we quoted in Chapter One that the Mashiach will not arrive until the "body" has been emptied of souls. This means that the final redemption cannot occur until all the souls that have been placed in the treasury of souls since the beginning of time incarnate into the world. This "body," or storehouse of souls, is essentially connected to how history develops and when certain types of souls enter the world, for history can be conceived as starting with the "head" and ending with the "feet." This perspective is alluded to in the phrase, "the footsteps of the Mashiach," or more literally, "the heels of the Mashiach," as the age immediately preceding the arrival of the Mashiach is referred to. Also, the term, "the end of days," alludes not only to the end of the six thousand year cycle, but can be understood as saying that the souls which will live in those days will originate from the "end," or "foot," of the "body." Rabbi Sutton explains that just like the brain directs all the movements of the body, both consciously and unconsciously, in a like manner the souls from Adam through the period of the Patriarchs and Matriarchs were from the head of the heavenly "body" and therefore their actions are archetypal in that they directed the unfolding of history and the manifold energies that appear and reappear in every generation. As history progresses, souls incarnate into this world from successively lower places of the heavenly "body," yet they are all still connected to the head. We can now understand a new perspective to the constant mention of the Patriarchs and Matriarchs in our prayers and rituals, for our bond to them is from the deepest soul connection.

A KABBALISTIC EXPLANATION OF THE HISTORICAL SOURCE OF JEWISH SOULS

The following section discusses perhaps the deepest and most revolutionary of all the revelations of the Arizal regarding reincarnation. Whereas in other teachings he reveals the soul history of individuals (to be discussed in the next chapter), here the Arizal reveals the soul history of the Jewish people as a whole. In doing so he illuminates not only the soul history of the nation of Israel, but lays forth an entirely different paradigm for the existential history of humankind. Embedded in these teachings is the background context behind many of the stories in the Torah and a new way of looking at the mission of the Jewish people.

These teachings are well-known by Kabbalists and students of Chassidut, but unlike many of the Arizal's teachings regarding cosmology, whose main ideas have entered into mainstream Jewish thought, these teachings have hovered closer to the borders of conventional Jewish consciousness. The reason is fairly clear – the revelations are groundbreaking and entail a paradigm shift of major proportions, and shifts of consciousness such as these are not easily accomplished. Nonetheless, the lessons and profound understandings implicit in the historical worldview the Arizal presents are too important to ignore. When looking deeply at the two paradigms he presented regarding cosmology and human history, we see that they parallel each other to a great degree. His line of thought in both cases, as we shall see, lead to the same conclusions.

What we present here then is a simplified version of a far more complex picture as transmitted by the Arizal to his students. For those wishing to, they can delve ever deeper into the sources, including *The Well of Living Waters* by Rabbi Abraham Sutton quoted above. We should keep in mind that the language of the Torah, the sages and especially the Kabbalah, is couched in highly symbolic and allegorical language, and both its literal description of reality, as well as its deeper meanings, are revealed only to those who can probe the inner and subtle implications contained in this enigmatic format. In addition, this can only be done within a framework of the cumulative oral Torah as transmitted throughout the generations.

Another very important comment is appropriate at this point, one that impacts highly on both this section and the entire next chapter. One of the most important of the thirteen rules by which we interpret the Torah (a listing of all thirteen rules can be found in the beginning section of the morning prayers) is *gezerah shavah*, which loosely translated means that similar words in different contexts are meant to clarify one another. This device is used hundreds of times in the Talmud to shed light on issues ranging from Jewish law to the alluded, allegorical, and mystical meaning of the text. Quite simply it is the way we "connect the dots" of Torah and thereby learn how to "connect the dots" of what we call the circumstances of our lives as well.

Gematria, Jewish numerology, works according to the same principle. In Hebrew each letter has a numerical equivalent. According to Kabbalah, if two words or phrases share the same number, they are considered to possess some significant connection. Gematria reveals a deeper set of correspondences than seen in the literal text and points to an entire mathematical structure underlying the Torah. As with physics and chemistry, which rest on mathematical foundations, so too the deeper dimensions of Torah become revealed and appreciated through gematria.

Yet it is not Kabbalah alone which employs gematria. The Talmud and Midrash also use this technique of learning in order to point out a cogent idea, and it has been used as well by a wide range of commentators throughout the ages, including Rashi. Inasmuch as Kabbalah seeks to make known the oneness of God and the interconnectedness of all reality, gematria assists by revealing these ideas through the very words and letters of the Torah text.

What we gain by using the learning techniques employed by the sages is a view of the deeper connections between verses and entire passages of the Torah. The Arizal, through intense study of the text, was granted from on High a new level of understanding how the dots connect throughout history as recounted in the Torah. By employing these methods he was additionally able to perceive the strands of reincarnation connecting different figures in the Torah, as will be discussed in greater depth in the next chapter.

As we have seen, Adam was an all-inclusive soul, containing all future souls within him. After the Torah records the story of Cain and Abel it states: "And Adam knew his wife again and she bore a son and she called his name Seth, for God has provided me another seed in place of Abel, for Cain had slain him." A few verses later we are told that Adam was one hundred thirty years old at the time Eve gave birth to Seth. It is explained that during those one hundred and thirty years Adam had no intimate relations with Eve but instead discharged wasted seed. Adam is an archetypal figure and every action of such a being has profound results. From this wasted seed an entire assortment of impure souls and un-rectified spirits were created.

This scenario according to Kabbalah and Chassidut is quite similar to the Arizal's teaching regarding the "breaking of the vessels," a major component of his cosmological explanation of the nature of reality, as discussed above. The primary purpose and mission of this world, olam hatikkun, is to rectify and redeem all the hidden sparks of light trapped in the shells of the broken vessels. This highly symbolic but accurate description of the fundamental existential essence of reality is mirrored in the sin of Adam and Eve in the Garden of Eden. Unable to manage the pure essence of the utopian existence in the Garden, which corresponds to the light in the Creation paradigm, their as yet immature "vessels" – their psychological, intellectual, and emotional states of consciousness – "broke." The result was their banishment from this utopian state. The exile from the Garden, the subsequent separation of Adam and Eve, and Adam discharging wasted seed become the parallel for the breaking of the vessels paradigm. The souls created from this seed were like the fallen shards of the broken vessels, each one containing a spark of light in need of great clarification and tikkun

The Arizal then reveals through connecting various words, verses, numerical correspondences, and stories in the book of Genesis how these un-rectified souls reincarnated in a number of generations – with each one possessing some kind of grievous flaw – until those souls that were ready for tikkun incarnated into the souls of the Jewish people in Egypt, who were entrusted with the mission of redeeming the sparks embedded deep in their souls, as well as of all reality. Those souls still not ready for tikkun were incarnated into the Egyptians (*Sha'ar Hapesukim, Parshat Shemot*). Throughout this process a few special souls, those of the Patriarchs and Matriarchs and their children, were able to lift themselves completely above the fallen state of their generation in order to begin the long and arduous task of repairing the consequences of the mistakes of Adam and Eve and their disastrous effects on all humanity.

These fallen souls were first incarnated in the generation of the flood. "The earth had become corrupt before God and the earth had become filled with robbery. And God saw the earth and behold it was corrupted, for all flesh had corrupted its way on the earth" (Genesis 6:11–12). Rashi explains that the word, "corrupt," alludes to sexual immorality. The fact that this word is used three times emphasizes the extent to which it had spread. According to the Arizal, the sexual immorality of the time of the flood is directly tied to the manner in which the souls of that generation came into being.

The second generation was that of the tower of Babel, when they conceived of building a tower to the heavens in order to do battle with God. "God descended to look at the city and tower which the sons of man [Adam] had built" (Genesis 11:5). Rashi comments that they are called the "sons of Adam" because just as Adam had exhibited a lack of appreciation and rebelled against God, so too did the generation of the dispersion lack appreciation for having been the descendants of Noah and his family who had escaped the flood, and also rebelled against God.

The Arizal understood more literally their being called "the sons of Adam" because their souls were directly tied to Adam emitting wasted seed. In fact, the literal translation is "the sons of *the* Adam," implying the first man. In relation to the generation of the flood it also connects them to Adam in the verse: "God saw the wickedness of man (Adam) was great on the earth..." (Genesis 6:5). Once again, the Arizal explains that this evil of man in the tenth generation from Adam was a direct result of the wasted seed of Adam.

The third time these souls were incarnated was in the days of the upheaval of Sodom. These souls were born into the people of Sodom, known for their cruelty and sexual immorality. Once more these un-rectified souls were drawn into sexual misconduct, a reflection of their own origin. After these three reincarnations the same souls were incarnated a fourth time in the land of Egypt, also known as the center of licentiousness in the world at that time. In this instance, though, the souls who through the generations had begun to lift themselves above the base desires of the lower soul were incarnated into the bodies of the emerging Jewish people, while those still immersed in their lower desires were incarnated into the Egyptians.

When Joseph rose to be the viceroy of Egypt he attempted to have all the Egyptians circumcised: "When all the land of Egypt hungered, the people cried out to Pharaoh for bread. So Pharaoh said to all Egypt, 'Go to Joseph; whatever he tells you, you should do'" (Genesis 41:55). Rashi in the name of *Midrash Tanchuma* explains the verse to mean that the people complained to Pharaoh regarding Joseph's request to circumcise themselves, to which Pharaoh replied that they should listen to what he says. The *Zohar* (2:17a) explains that Joseph desired to "convert" those souls who were ready to leave the depraved ways of Egypt. In a wider sense, he wanted to begin the process of rectifying the fallen souls from Adam through circumcising the male organ of reproduction. Although his motives were pure they were premature, leading to the very opposite. These "converted" souls became the "mixed multitude" that Moses insisted on taking with them when the Jews left Egypt. God warned him that these souls were not yet ready to be totally redeemed, that they needed one more incarnation, but Moses, who included in his soul an aspect of Adam, felt impelled to rectify these fallen sparks. His motives were also well intended but in retrospect he came to see that God was of course correct, as these were the people primarily responsible for the sin of the Golden Calf.

A slightly different record of the incarnating souls produced by the emitted seed of Adam is presented in the commentary on the Passover Haggadah, *Shem Mishmuel*, in a remarkable piece entitled "The Matter of the Four Cups," which explains the profound wisdom behind the Rabbinic injunction to drink four cups of wine on Passover night. Here, *Shem Mishmuel* inserts an additional generation, considering the Age of Enosh to be the first period in which the un-rectified souls incarnated. The Age of Enosh is infamous for being the time when the seeds of idol worship were initially planted. The seeds of idol worship were actually sown by Adam and Eve when they distanced themselves from God, as symbolized by their attempt to hide from God after eating of the Tree of Knowledge of Good and Evil (Genesis 3:8). When a person is focused on the gratification of his or her own desires and on self-worship, and are thus detached from holiness or Godliness – as when they ate from the forbidden tree, or when Adam separated from his wife and discharged seed for one hundred thirty years – the leap to idol worship is not far. In any event, by inserting another stage, he has reckoned the incarnation of these souls in Egypt to be the fifth generation.

Shem Mishmuel explains the correspondence between the first four generations in which these souls incarnated and the fifth one, when they returned in the emerging Jewish people, at great length through a series of associated topics, each having four basic components or levels plus a fifth component or level that is intrinsically connected to the first four. This, he taught, parallels the Rabbinic injunction to drink four cups on Passover night, as well as the custom of pouring a fifth cup for Elijah the Prophet. Rabbi Yitzchak Ginsburgh explains that this seeming contradiction as to whether the Jews in Egypt were the fourth or fifth generation of incarnated souls from the spilt seed of Adam can be understood by how the generation of Enosh is sometimes treated as a separate and distinct generation and at other times is subsumed in the general treatment of the ten generations beginning with Adam and culminating with Noah.

The Arizal in *Sha'ar Hapesukim* (*Parshat Shemot*) explained that two of the punishments that the people of Israel suffered in Egypt were directly connected to their failings in previous incarnations. "Pharaoh commanded the entire people, saying, 'Every son that will be born, into the river you shall throw him, and every daughter will be kept alive'" (Exodus 1:22). The decree to drown all the baby boys in Egypt was connected to the generation of the flood and their wantonly emitting seed, which the Arizal figuratively compared to allowing their seed to "drown." These acts led to the drowning of their incarnations by the Egyptians. That it was only the boys and not the girls that were so punished is due ultimately to it being Adam who originally discharged his seed in a wasteful manner.

The other punishment of the people of Israel was to work with mortar and bricks: "The Egyptians enslaved the children of Israel with cruel harshness. They embittered their lives with hard work, with mortar and bricks…" (Exodus 1:13–14). According to the Arizal this relates back to the building of the tower of Babel: "They said one to the other, 'Come let us make bricks and burn them in fire'; and the brick served them as stone and the lime served them as mortar" (Genesis 11:3). The bricks burnt in fire relate to the heat of passion experienced by Adam when wantonly wasting seed.

According to the *Zohar*, Abraham was an incarnation of Adam and he and the other Patriarchs and Matriarchs were the first to begin a fundamental tikkun for Adam and Eve. At the "Covenant of the Pieces" God revealed to Abraham the future of the Jewish people: "Know with certainty that your offspring [literally, seed] will be strangers in a land not their own, they will enslave them [i.e., your children will be slaves] and they will oppress them for four hundred years…. And the fourth generation shall return here…" (Genesis 15:13–16). The Arizal explains that Abraham, as an incarnation of Adam, is being told that it is his emitted seed that will go down to Egypt. It can be understood that the four hundred years or four generations allude to the tikkun that will begin to occur in Egypt for the four generations in which the souls of the emitted seed were incarnated but as a whole could not rectify themselves.

This perspective sheds light on why Abraham prayed to save Sodom despite knowing how wicked they had become, for deep inside he knew holy sparks were entrapped there needing to be uplifted and purified. In addition, he felt a certain conscious or unconscious responsibility as those sparks were contained inside souls that were an incarnation of the seed of Adam, who was now incarnated in himself. In the end, Lot and his daughters were saved. According to tradition, the soul of Ruth comes from the incestuous relations between Lot and his daughters, and from Ruth comes the lineage of King David, who is the progenitor of the Mashiach. It was this spark specifically that Abraham intuitively knew he needed to save.

Another amazing connection the Arizal made when "connecting the dots" was the number, one hundred thirty, which first appears when describing the birth of Seth after the one hundred thirty years of Adam's separation from his wife. Moses, according to tradition, was born when his mother Jochebed was one hundred thirty years old. Moses, as we will learn in the next chapter, was a reincarnation of both Abel and Seth. It was around the time of Moses' birth that Pharaoh was correctly informed by his astrologers that a redeemer was to be imminently born to the Jews, to which he responded by decreeing that all newborn males should be killed. They also saw correctly that the redeemer would be judged by water, but erred in thinking it would be by drowning. Later, Moses was denied permission to enter the Promised Land for striking the rock to bring forth water, rather than speaking to it as he was commanded by God.

A most fascinating connection involving the number one hundred thirty arises from the gifts that the princes brought when dedicating the Tabernacle at the beginning of the forty-year sojourn in the desert. The Tabernacle was dedicated on the first day of Nisan, the day the world was created, as the Talmud explains God to have created the world in thought in Tishrei (the date we refer to as "Rosh Hashanah") and in deed in Nisan (*Rosh Hashanah* 11a). According to the Midrash the dedication of the

Tabernacle was the greatest day since the very inception of the world. One can imagine the excitement, anticipation, and energy surrounding this awesome event. The Torah describes how each of the tribal princes brought an assortment of gifts to be used in the Tabernacle (Numbers 7:1–89). Interestingly enough, they all brought the very same gifts, but we are told by the Midrash that each one had a completely different intent when offering their gifts.

In his explanation of the dedication ceremony, Rashi brings one set of intentions, those of Nachshon, the prince of the tribe of Judah, the first to bring the gifts (Numbers 7:19–23). These explanations are practically unique in the commentary of Rashi, as they use an assortment of Kabbalistic methods and devices that are only rarely used by him in explaining the simple meaning of the text. The fact that these methods are employed here in such a concentrated way alerts us to the fact that very deep meanings are certainly alluded to in the text. When enumerating these gifts according to Rashi's explanations we see immediately that the intentions here begin with Adam and go through central events in history till the time of the dedication.

We will now review these gifts in the order they were given, along with Rashi's explanation, and then try to shed light on the spiritual intent of Nachshon and its relevance to the Arizal's paradigm of history, as well as the underlying theme to his teachings:

** "A silver bowl weighing 130 shekels": The numerical value of "silver bowl" in Hebrew is 930, corresponding to the years of Adam's life, while 130 corresponds to the age at which Adam and Eve gave birth to Seth.

** "One silver basin weighing seventy shekels": The numerical value of "one silver basin" is 520, corresponding to Noah's age of 500 when he gave birth to his children, and 20 for the years before he began to give birth that God told him of the coming flood. The weight of seventy corresponds to the seventy nations that descend from Noah, those who were involved in the tower of Babel.

** "One ladle weighing ten shekels full of incense": "One ladle" represents the totality of Torah, given by the One God. The weight of ten represents the Ten Commandments, the seminal teachings of the entire Torah. The word for "incense" equals 613, the number of commandments in the Torah when the letters are interchanged according to *Atbash*, a little known Kabbalistic alphabet.

** "One bull": This alludes to Abraham who fed a bull to the angels who came to announce the impending birth of a son.

** "One ram": This hints to the ram that was taken by Abraham in place of sacrificing his son Isaac.

** "One sheep": This alludes to the sheep of Laban that Jacob was able to breed in an ingenious manner in order that they would become his sheep, according to an agreement he had made with Laban.

** "One goat": In order to atone for the sale of Joseph by his brothers. A goat was used in particular for the brothers had dipped his special cloak in the blood of a goat to trick Jacob into thinking Joseph was dead.

** "Two cattle for peace offerings": This corresponds to Moses and Aaron who brought peace between God and Israel.

** "Five rams, five male goats, and five sheep": These three sets of animals correspond to Israel, who are divided into three divisions – *kohanim* (priests), *levi'im* (Levites), and Israelites, as well as the three divisions of the Bible – Torah, Prophets, and Writings. The number five also corresponds to the five books of Moses and the five commandments that were written on each of the two tablets that Moses brought down from Mt. Sinai.

We see from these explanations that Nachshon was trying to connect his intentions in bringing the gifts to the spirit of the day – that of tikkun and revelation. The dedication of the Tabernacle represented the culmination of the process of repentance for the sin of the Golden Calf and symbolized God's acceptance of the people's atonement. In addition, the dedication represented the fulfillment of the purpose of creation – the creation of a permanent dwelling place for God in the lower worlds, and more important, in the hearts and minds of the Jewish people.

With that in mind, Nachshon's gifts were intended to rectify the combined history of the world, as well as draw down upon the people the spiritual energy of the great deeds of the righteous individuals and the Patriarchs who preceded them. What better time to rectify the sin of Adam and Eve, of the generation of the flood, the building of the tower of Babel by the descendants of Noah, and the selling of Joseph which led to our descent into Egypt. What better opportunity to draw upon themselves the spirit of self-sacrifice of Abraham and Isaac, the wisdom of Jacob, the peace between God and Israel brought about by Moses and Aaron, and the commitment to the 613 mitzvot of the Torah.

We must remember also that Nachshon was the one who jumped into the sea until the water reached his nostrils before it split in front of the Jews as they were being pursued by the advancing Egyptians. His act represents the courage to confront all obstacles, trusting in the word of God, Who told Moses to tell the people to go forward. We see again in his holy intentions at the time of the dedication his desire to grasp the moment in order to mend the world from the results of its sins and shortcomings.

There is a great lesson here for every individual. There are times in our lives when events and circumstances align themselves in such a way that by taking the initiative and tuning in to the opportunity that is presenting itself, truly great tikkunim can be made.

For example: two people who have been quarreling for a long time find themselves in a situation where they need to cooperate and work together, or where the joyous or conducive spirit of an occasion allows them to drop their defenses and reach out to each other. Many times a new job, changing location, or a new relationship, opens us up to fresh energy and a new start in life. At other times, a crisis situation creates the opportunity to look at things differently or to take serious stock of one's actions. At each of these junctures a person with the right intent can in a relatively short time fix and heal his or her past and break through to a new future by adopting a new, wholesome attitude about life.

This same idea holds true for history as well. At the time of the Exodus the opportunity for true tikkun was present as never before. Due to the spiritual work of our Patriarchs, Matriarchs, and the twelve tribes, the sparks of holiness trapped in the discharged seed of Adam were ready to receive their initial rectification by becoming the Jewish people. Receiving the Torah fifty days after leaving Egypt became the guiding light for the ultimate redemption of all the holy sparks trapped in the wasted seed of Adam and the broken vessels of Creation.

On an even grander scale, the possibility always exists for the entire world to be confronted with events and circumstances that will create a radically new situation, and with it the chance for permanent change in how the world conducts its affairs and in how nations relate to each other. The words of the prophets reverberate with allusion and they prophesy of occurrences that will usher in the Messianic era. Then, and only then, will the full repair and healing of the world occur.

When Nachshon brought his gifts, his thoughts were in tune with the energy of newness, repair, and atonement inherent in that day. How much he and the other princes were able to accomplish we may never know, but their example is a beacon of light to what we can attempt in our own lives.

This is the message embedded in the teachings of reincarnation and cosmology as taught by the Arizal. Although they, like much of the Torah, are masked in highly symbolic and allegorical language, not only does it not detract from their relevant wisdom, it accentuates their ultimate truth and reality. The underlying theme of both the "breaking of the vessels" and the unique view of history presented by the Arizal is of tikkun. The history of the Jewish people has been spent in good part scattered among the nations. The Arizal explains that this is part of the Divine plan, as the mission of the Jewish people is to identify the holy sparks trapped throughout all reality and to clarify, uplift, and transform them. Their full redemption will take place as the Jewish people return to the Land of Israel, where all these holy sparks will create a critical mass of positive, holy energy that will draw the soul of the Mashiach into the world.

THE MASHIACH AND THE CULMINATION OF HISTORY

In the previous section we made mention of the fact that the spark of the Mashiach's soul comes from the evil place of Sodom and the incestuous relationship between Lot and his daughters. We see from the text and the commentary of Rashi that the daughters of Lot, having just experienced the total destruction of Sodom and the surrounding area, feared that the entire world had been destroyed and that only they remained (Genesis 19:31–32). Sleeping with their father was in their eyes the only chance they had to continue the human race (*Horayot* 10b).

It is known that the strange circumstances in this story are not unique in the lineage leading to King David, from whom the Mashiach will descend. Judah, the son of Jacob and the progenitor of David's tribe, was also involved in an extraordinary situation in which he unknowingly slept with his daughter-in-law Tamar, from whom came the seed of David (Genesis 38:1–30). Ruth, a convert, who descended from the relationship of Lot and one of his daughters, was likewise involved in a story of intrigue leading up to her marriage to Boaz (see the Book of Ruth). Finally, David himself was born under controversial circumstances and due to this was "exiled" to be a shepherd in the field. When Samuel was instructed to anoint one of the sons of Jesse as king he was presented with all seven of Jesse's sons, none of whom turned out to be the intended one. Only when Samuel pressed was he told of the last "son" who was off in the fields with the flocks. (For a more detailed explanation of the convoluted nature of the lineage of King David see the overview of the ArtScroll Book of Ruth.)

The unusual situations in all these stories are very consistent with what we have learned, for deeply hidden in the exterior shells of reality are the highest sparks of light and holiness. When a wall topples, the stones from the top fall farthest from the base. Souls like those of King David or the Mashiach come into the world to redeem the holiest of sparks from the very lowest realms. Therefore, these stories all have a common thread whereby the spark of the Mashiach had to be revealed through the most questionable of circumstances, for according to the Arizal the forces of negativity and opposition present in the world would never willingly accede to holiness being so easily revealed or redeemed. The ancestors of the Mashiach, therefore, had to come into the world through the "back door," as it were.

Another reason the soul of the Mashiach needs to come from the very depths of the klipot, the impure shells of the broken vessels, is that this is his ultimate task – to enlighten, heal, reveal, and redeem all the fallen sparks of reality. Since his own soul will be extracted from these low places, he will know and understand them intimately. It will give him the ability to relate to and inspire all those souls needing to raise themselves to a higher level of consciousness. This, as the Arizal has taught us, is in fact the mission of the world in general and of the Jewish people in particular. It is explained that the last word of the account of Creation (Genesis 2:3) – "which God created *to make*" – seems to be superfluous. Kabbalah and Chassidut explain that the word "to make" means "to rectify." God purposefully left the work of finishing the process of Creation in the hands of man, who is meant through free choice to partner with God in the rectification of the world. It is further pointed out that the last letters of the three concluding words of the narrative of Creation – "that God created to make" – spell the word *emet*, "truth," prompting the sages to remark that God's seal is truth, since these words are the seal (i.e., the closing words) of Creation. These two ideas combine to emphasize an important truth – that man is enjoined to be partners with God in the ongoing saga of creation and especially of rectifying all reality.

At the beginning of this chapter we discussed the idea of history being like a body. In the early generations souls originated, as it were, from the head of this "body." As history developed the souls came from successively lower parts of the body, till at the time right before the culmination of history in the Messianic era they will come from the feet, a time termed, "the heels of the Mashiach." We also mentioned the Talmudic teaching that the Mashiach will not arrive before all the souls "leave the body," the heavenly treasury of souls. As we approach the year 6,000 (at the time of this writing we are in the year 5768 in the Jewish calendar) the process of emptying the body of souls has dramatically accelerated. In the last two hundred years the world's population has increased at an astonishing rate. This is a result of the world being readied for the Messianic era. The implication of this is astounding – all the souls who have ever incarnated at different times of history and in all sorts of different soul combinations are all coming together on earth at the same time. This is one of the reasons life appears to be so complex in contemporary times, as there is simply an overload of psychic, emotional, and spiritual energy in need of processing. Different parts of our soul histories are all returning at the same time in an increasingly interconnected physical and spiritual global village.

It also means that the sum total of human intellect has never been greater, as can be seen in the phenomenal changes that began with the industrial revolution and continued by leaps and bounds through the incredible advances in science, communications, medicine, and transportation. The stage is being set for even further changes in both the material and spiritual realms, such as we can barely imagine.

One of the critical factors in this quickly unfolding drama is the rebirth of Israel as a sovereign nation. It is no coincidence that after nearly two thousand years of dispersion and oppression we are witnessing at this juncture in time the ingathering of the exiles to their ancient homeland. There is no precedent in all history for such an occurrence.

According to the historical paradigm of the Arizal, the Jews were scattered to the four corners of the earth in order to gather the sparks of holiness and light dispersed among the nations and bring them home to Israel. Rabbi Abraham Isaac Kook, the first chief Rabbi of Palestine during the British Mandate, spoke and wrote extensively about this phenomenon and how we were witnessing in the rebirth of Israel not only a political and historical event of major proportions, but a spiritual and mystical occurrence as well. This was predicted by all of the Jewish prophets throughout the ages, that in the "end of days," at the time of the Messianic era, God would gather the Jews together in Israel.

We are living in truly awesome times; the speed of change within both the material world, as well as spiritual revelations regarding the secrets of the Torah, is staggering. Jewish teachings of reincarnation, cosmology, and history fit into the overall wisdom preparing the world for even more spectacular discoveries to come. Contemplating our soul roots and spiritual journey throughout the ages can play a very positive and energizing force in our lives in the here and now as we navigate ourselves through the multifaceted world we live in. In this way we can repair the past manifest in the present, in order to rectify the future.

CHAPTER SIX:

Portraits and Soul Histories

$\mathcal{A}$long with the traditions relating to the general principles and dynamics of reincarnation transmitted by the Arizal to his students, he passed on a virtual "who's who" of reincarnated individuals who appear in the Bible, as well as sages from the time of the Mishnah and the Talmud. These fascinating insights are spread throughout the *Kitvei Ha'ari*, the eight volumes of the teachings of the Arizal, arranged and edited by Rabbi Chaim Vital, his primary student. The most concentrated place of these revelations is of course in the *Sha'ar Hagilgulim* ("Gate of Reincarnations").

In the first chapter of this book we mentioned how Rabbi Menachem Azarya of Fano, a student of Rabbi Yisrael Sarouk, who was among the close circle of students of the Arizal, compiled a relatively short book entitled *Gilgulei Neshamot* ("Reincarnation of Souls"). This very important book organizes, in alphabetical order, the specific gilgulim of individuals as revealed by the Arizal. The notes, compiled by Rabbi Yerucham Meir Lainer, the son of the great Chassidic Rebbe of Ishbitz, bring additional Kabbalistic traditions as well.

The vast majority of these revelations, as we mentioned in the last chapter, are based on comparing the details of biblical stories with the oral traditions recorded in the Midrash, *Zohar*, and Talmud, in order to "connect the dots" between souls. It took someone like the Arizal who was granted unusual powers of insight from Above to reveal so much of what had been hidden until then. There is no doubt though that previous sages knew some of these traditions, which were included in a subtle and coded fashion in various Rabbinic and Kabbalistic texts.

Before delving into this area, we preface this section with the words of Rabbi Lainer who, in his introduction to *Gilgulei Neshamot*, wrote about the importance of the wisdom the volume contained (Menachem Azarya of Fano, *Reincarnation of Souls*, trans. Avraham Lider, with a commentary by Yerucham Meir Lainer [Jerusalem: Machon Haktav, 2001], p. xii):

> "When examining the words of this book it appears that his intention was to increase our consciousness and awareness of how a person's reincarnation can be identified through his deeds and machinations, to recognize the quarry his soul was excavated from, to assess the damage previously done, and to discover why the soul was forced to come a second time and dwell among the living, so that we learn these secrets and make them known, thereby healing the past. We will thus learn how to correct the roots of our souls which were damaged in previous years, and also how we must act in the days to come. For a man must ponder these matters profoundly…to see how former beings corrected their souls in the past. Each man must study himself, so as to learn and understand his characteristics and his habits. As a result, he will see where they lead him and know what his source is. He will then know in which reincarnation he presently is, what he did in the past, and how he sinned, thereby improving his deeds in this latter life, so that he need not die again."

Although most people do not merit knowing the details of previous gilgulim in their own background, realizing that gilgul exists and studying the soul histories of other people should provide positive direction in accomplishing those repairs needed in our own lives. The Arizal did not reveal a "who's who" of biblical characters for intellectual entertainment, but to make known how the dynamics of gilgul operates using real people so that we draw the proper lessons for the present.

The specific revelations of the Arizal need to be viewed in the context of a broader understanding of each person's complete soul history. For the most part, he did not leave us with an exact soul history of individuals, rather fragments of insight. In some cases the various parts of the total story can be pieced together to form a chain of gilgulim through many generations. It takes a good deal of thought, though, to put the puzzle of soul histories together.

To say that one person was reincarnated into another person in a different lifetime means, according to the Arizal, that a certain aspect of a person's soul is reborn into another person. In the notes to the text and in a careful analysis of the various traditions, it can be seen that in many cases a number of soul sparks of different people were concurrently reincarnated into one person. This confirms what we have already pointed out – that one person may contain a number of different souls simultaneously, not to mention how a person may be "impregnated" by various souls as well.

We will now review in very brief form some of these fascinating insights, which when fully considered give us an entirely new perspective on many biblical characters and stories. In addition, we will focus our attention on a few individuals to explore the profound connections revealed when understanding the associations that exist among people of the same or different generations, and the complex soul configurations of individuals. The cases we chose highlight many of the various dynamics and principles, including some of the underlying reasons, of reincarnation discussed throughout the book. For those seeking additional cases, they are encouraged to investigate the book, *Gilgulei Neshamot*, and the original teachings of the Arizal.

WOMEN

When discussing women and reincarnation in the last chapter we explained that the Arizal does mention throughout his teachings various gilgulim of women, sometimes in relation to their husbands and sometimes with no mention of their husbands at all.

** We learned in the last chapter how numerous souls emanate from the same soul spark. In the 116th entry of *Reincarnation of Souls*, Rabbi Menachem Azarya lists different souls that all originate in the same spark. It is very significant that Eve and all four Matriarchs – Sarah, Rebecca, Rachel, and Leah all come from the same spark. This confirms the idea that all the Matriarchs worked at rectifying the sin of Eve.

** Two different souls reincarnated into Deborah, the judge and prophetess. The first was that of Tamar who, motivated by a prophetic vision that kings would issue from a union between her and Judah's family, took the initiative to have a son from that family by disguising herself as a prostitute when Judah would not allow his last son to marry her. Unknowingly, Judah slept with her and Perez, the product of that intimate moment, was the first in the line from which King David would later descend (Genesis 38:1–30). In the book of Judges (4:5) it describes Deborah: "And she sat under the palm tree (*tomer*) of Devorah." The word for "palm tree" in this verse, *tomer*, an alternate form for *tamar*, is according to the Arizal an allusion to Tamar being reincarnated in Deborah. The reason she would sit under the palm tree was in order to rectify her sitting at the crossroads in the guise of a prostitute. Even though her intentions were good and she was considered righteous, nonetheless, there was a certain repair that needed to be made for the appearance of being a prostitute (*Reincarnation of Souls* #139).

The other soul who incarnated into Deborah was Zipporah, the wife of Moses. When Moses was sent back to Egypt to participate in the exodus, Zipporah initially accompanied him on the way. At some point, however, Moses sent her back to her home and so she was not present when Israel sang the Song of the Sea after their miraculous rescue, and this caused her pain. In the merit of having circumcised her son, an act which took initiative and great courage, she incarnated into Deborah, who was also an unusually strong-willed woman and leader. After the latter led the defeat of Sisera's army, inspired by the spirit of prophecy, she broke into singing one of the ten archetypal songs of Creation. This time Zipporah was able to participate.

The connection between Zipporah and Deborah is further alluded to at the beginning of the song of Deborah when it says: "In time of tumultuous strife [*bifro'a pera'ot*]…" (Judges 5:2). The root letters of both these words are the same as *periah*, the part of circumcision when the membrane is removed, alluding to Zipporah circumcising her son (*Reincarnation of Souls* #152).

** Judith, the brave woman who entered the camp of the Greeks in order to break the siege around Jerusalem, was the soul of Jael, another brave woman who killed Sisera, at the time of the war Deborah fought. In order to kill him, Jael first gave him milk to drink and then, according to the Talmud, she slept with him. When he had finally fallen asleep she took a tent peg and drove it through his temple (Judges 4:19). When discussing this incident the Talmud states that even though she committed a sin by sleeping with him, since her intentions were righteous she is judged favorably (*Horayot* 10b). Nonetheless, in order to rectify the blemish of sleeping with Sisera she incarnated into Judith, who fed a Greek general dairy products, like Jael, and then some wine till he fell asleep, but this time she did not sleep with him, she merely cut off his head and escaped from the camp. When the head of the general was placed on display on the walls of the city the shocked Greek troops fled and the siege was broken. In this way the blemish of Jael was rectified by Judith (*Reincarnation of Souls* #65).

** The wife of On ben Pelet, whose sound advice at the time of the insurrection of Korah against Moses saved her husband (Numbers 16:1–35; *Sanhedrin* 109b), incarnated into Tzellofanit, the mother of Samson, while On incarnated into Samson's father. Since she saved her husband in a previous lifetime, Tzellofanit merited to be the first to be visited by the angel who told her of the special son they would have (Judges 13:2–25; *Reincarnation of Souls* #120).

** Naomi, the mother-in-law of Ruth, had a spark of the Matriarch Leah, while Ruth had a spark of the Matriarch Rachel, her sister in a previous lifetime. When Jacob was ready to marry Rachel, her father, Laban, decided to switch Leah and Rachel. So that Leah would not be humiliated, Rachel gave her the special signs she had made with Jacob, who suspected that Laban might try to deceive him (*Megilla* 13b). Therefore, it says, "And Ruth clung to her" (Ruth 1:14). When Ruth gave birth to Obed she suddenly disappears from the text and the child is referred to as the son of Naomi. This is because Obed was the soul of Judah, who in a previous lifetime was Leah's son, Leah now being incarnated into Naomi (*Reincarnation of Souls* #98).

** In the early generations of Genesis, Lemech is described as having two wives: Adah, with whom he had children, and Zillah, who was made to drink a contraceptive potion in order not to get pregnant, although she did conceive and give birth later in life. Lemech reincarnated into Elkanah who also had two wives. Peninnah, who had many children, was the incarnation of Adah; Hannah, who had no children, was an incarnation of Zillah. Hannah prayed from the depths of her heart to have a child and her prayer was answered when she gave birth to Samuel, the future prophet. His birth and her fervent prayer were the healing for drinking the contraceptive (*Reincarnation of Souls* #80).

** When the Matriarch Sarah could not bear children she suggested to Abraham that he take her handmaiden, Hagar, as a wife. When Hagar became pregnant immediately, she took to belittling Sarah. Hagar was reincarnated into the handmaiden of Jesse, the father of David, who had separated from his wife out of concern for a newly published court ruling which would prohibit him from being with her. He sought then to have relations with his handmaiden, but she reported his intentions to his spouse, leading to Jesse unwittingly sleeping with his own wife. David was born from that union. In this way Hagar received her tikkun (*Reincarnation of Souls* #47).

** Bat Shua, the wife of Judah, returns in Bat Sheva, the wife of David, who is an incarnation of Judah. Here, as in many other examples, we see husbands and wives in one life returning together in another life as well. Just as Tamar was worthy to give birth to kings through her union with Judah, so too was Bat Shua worthy to give birth to kings, but because of her son's evil ways she did not merit that in her previous lifetime. Therefore she was incarnated into Bat Sheva, who did not resist David, and in a sense did what Tamar had done with Judah in order to give birth to kings. Ultimately it was her son Solomon who inherited the kingship from David (*Reincarnation of Souls* #29).

** Bat Sheva, the wife of King David, was reincarnated in the soul of Beruria, the wife of Rabbi Meir. Just as Bat Sheva acted as a close counsel to her husband, Beruria would occasionally teach the students of her husband. When David took Bat Sheva, he contrived a way for her husband Uriah to be killed in battle. Uriah's soul then reincarnated into the soul of one of Rabbi Meir's students, who attempted to seduce Beruria. She became so distraught by her own actions that she killed herself. Bat Sheva was the cause of Uriah's death, and now he was the cause of Beruriah's death (*Reincarnation of Souls* #35).

** The wife of Korah, who goaded him on to rebel against Moses, was reincarnated into Jezebel, the wife of the king, Ahab. She had a chance to rectify her evil ways but once again fell into the same trap of doing evil (*Reincarnation of Souls* #5).

** We began this section discussing the Matriarchs' attempt to rectify the sin of Eve. According to tradition women perform three specific mitzvot in order to rectify Eve's sin of eating from the Tree of Knowledge of Good and Evil, which brought death into the world. The three mitzvot and the reason women do them are: *challah*, the tithe taken from dough when baking bread, because Eve brought death to the man who was created from the dust of the earth and symbolically kneaded into a human being (see Rashi on Genesis 2:6); *niddah*, guarding the laws of family purity in regard to the monthly cycle of menstruation and intimate marital relations, because she figuratively spilled man's blood; and *hadlaka*, lighting candles to usher in Shabbat and holidays, as she symbolically put out the soul of man which is compared to light, as in the verse: "The candle of God is the soul of man (Proverbs 20:27). The first letters of these three words spell *Channah* (Hannah). Sarah was a reincarnation of Eve and was the first to strive to rectify the original sin. The Midrash states that in Sarah's tent a lamp burned from Shabbat to Shabbat, her dough was blessed, and a cloud – a sign of the Divine Presence – hovered over her tent, which exuded holiness and purity (*Genesis Rabba* 60:16). This Midrash indicates that Sarah observed these three mitzvot, and her tent was blessed accordingly. The Arizal states that although she rectified these three mitzvot she did so in a very general way and it still required three other women to rectify them more specifically: the Zarephathi woman who sustained Elijah the Prophet with a miraculous jar of flour parallels challah (1 Kings

17:13); Hannah, who was childless but through her impassioned prayer merited to give birth to Samuel the Prophet, parallels niddah (1 Samuel 1:1–28); and the Shunamite woman, who cared for Elisha the Prophet by preparing for him a room with a bed, table, chair, and lamp, parallels *hadlaka* (2 Kings 4:10). Jewish women throughout the generations have continued to focus their deep intent on the continuing clarification of these three mitzvot, which according to the Arizal is part of the overall rectification of Eve and the ongoing cycles of reincarnation dating back to her children.

MEN

** After the flood, Noah planted a vineyard and eventually became drunk from the wine produced from the grapes. The *Zohar* explains that as he faced a new world and a new beginning, he was trying to rectify Adam's eating of the Tree of Knowledge of Good and Evil, which many identify as being a grape vine. Noah's getting drunk represents his failed attempt. As a result of his being drunk he was disgraced in his nakedness, and according to some he was castrated. He received his tikkun through Joseph who refrained from drinking wine despite all his troubles, until he drank wine with his brothers. A further tikkun in the realm of sexuality was made in his ability to withstand the advances of the wife of Potifar, a repair of Noah's sexual disgrace (*Reincarnation of Souls* #153).

** According to the *Zohar* (3:103a), Canaan, who was cursed to be a slave to his brothers by his grandfather, Noah, for his part in humiliating or castrating him (Genesis 9:22–25), returned in Eliezer, the servant of Abraham. As the servant of Abraham he reached great heights of spirituality through his loyalty and humbleness. In the merit of his rectified characteristics, and due to his selflessness in finding a wife for Isaac, he underwent a spiritual transformation, and according to the *Zohar*, was transformed from one who was cursed to one who is blessed. Here is a beautiful example of how previous lifetimes affect a person's circumstances in life, but do not impinge on his free will to dramatically change and rectify the soul. Eliezer was reincarnated into Eliezer the son of Moses, and according to Chassidic tradition, he further reincarnated into Eliezer, the father of the Ba'al Shem Tov (see Yitzchak Ginsburgh, *Kabbalah and Meditation for the Nations* [Jerusalem: Gal Einai, 2006], pp. 137–8).

** Despite Joseph being able to withstand the wife of Potifar, the Talmud relates that his passion was so aroused that ten drops of semen were excreted through his ten fingers (*Sotah* 36b). Although we mentioned in Chapter One that the Arizal taught on one occasion that Joseph's ten brothers returned in the ten martyrs at the time of the Romans, on another occasion he taught that the soul sparks of the ten martyrs came from these ten drops of semen. Joseph himself was reincarnated in Phineas who was jealous to protect the covenant of sexual purity when Zimri, a prince of Simon, audaciously took a Midianite woman to his tent. Phineas killed both of them and by his action stopped a horrendous plague that had begun to spread throughout the camp. Through this act of zealousness his passion for the wife of Potifar was completely rectified.

** A spark of the soul of Joseph also returned in Joshua who later married Rahab, the woman who helped Israel conquer the city of Jericho. The wife of Potifar had a holy side and an impure side. Her desire for Joseph was a mixture of the two. She was driven by both raw desire and a deep soul attraction to the holiness of Joseph. Rahab is said to be the soul of Potifar's wife from her good side (*Reincarnation of Souls* #90).

** In a series of teachings in the Mishnah (*Sotah* 1:8) regarding "a measure for a measure," it is stated that Absalom, King David's rebellious son, was proud of his hair, and thus he stumbled because of his hair – he was killed when his hair became so entangled in a tree he could not escape those that pursued him. Absalom, who was very handsome, was reincarnated into another good-looking young man who became a *nazir*, one who vows to let his hair grow without cutting it. One time when looking at his reflection, his evil inclination made him feel proud and haughty regarding his beautiful hair. In response he rebuked his evil inclination and cut off his hair for the sake of Heaven (*Nedarim* 9a; *Nazir* 4b). This act was considered a tikkun for the pride Absalom took in his beauty and his hair (*Reincarnation of Souls* #20). It further states that the soul of Absalom was a spark of the son from the initial un-rectified union of David and Bat Sheva, who died immediately after birth, which accounts for the troubles he caused his father by rebelling against him (*Reincarnation of Souls* #22).

** At the time when Pharaoh decreed that all the male children should be drowned in the Nile River, Amram, the leader of the generation, separated from his wife in order not to have more children. His daughter Miriam gently rebuked him arguing that Pharaoh's decree was just against the males, while his separating from his wife was, in effect, a decree against females as well, especially since the entire generation followed his lead. Taking to heart his daughter's words, he remarried his wife and as a result Moses was born (*Sotah* 12a). Amram's soul returned in King Hezekiah, who was faced with a similar predicament. Hezekiah entered into a deep state of Divine revelation and saw that his children would all be worthless, so he decided not to have children. The prophet Isaiah came and rebuked him saying that he should focus on performing the mitzvah of procreation, and that he should not get involved in God's accounting of who will be worthy and who will be worthless (*Berachot* 10a). The discussion of these soul connections continues with the verse of Isaac smelling the scent of the Garden of Eden in the clothes of Jacob when he is pretending to be Esau (see Rashi on Genesis 27:27). The Talmud (*Sanhedrin* 37a) comments that one can also read the word "his clothes" as "his betrayers," for in the future even traitors will smell good, as God finds ways "that no one will be lost to Him." The Midrash explains that this refers to two sinners at the time of the Second Temple who were traitors but later repented (*Genesis Rabba* 65:22). It is interesting to note that Hezekiah ended up marrying the daughter of Isaiah. Their son Manasseh did indeed perpetrate much evil during his reign, yet he also ended up repenting for his grave actions. His grandson, Josiah, was considered one of the most righteous of the kings.

** Jacob and Esau were not only twin brothers but they were archetypal rivals, as was revealed to Rebecca when they were still in her womb: "The children agitated within her, and she said, 'If so, why am I thus?' And she went to inquire of God. And God said to her: 'Two nations are in your womb; two regimes from your insides shall be separated; the might shall pass from one regime to the other, and the elder shall serve the younger'" (Genesis 25: 22–23). This rivalry was renewed when the Jews were in exile in Persia, as recorded in the Scroll of Esther. Mordecai was a reincarnation of Jacob, and Haman, who wanted to wipe out the Jewish people, was a reincarnation of Esau. Jacob, after receiving the blessing from Isaac, fled his home when Esau sought to kill him. When he confronted Esau once again after thirty-four years, he bowed down to him seven times. Although many commentators explain that he did so from a position of strength, especially after defeating Esau's angel the night before in the archetypal battle when Jacob merited the new name of Israel, nonetheless, others see this as a blemish on Jacob's soul. When they meet again as Mordecai and Haman, Mordecai refuses to bow to Haman, which triggered the latter's desire to annihilate the Jewish people. In the end, Mordecai was able to rise above Haman, thus rectifying Jacob's bowing down to Esau (*Reincarnation of Souls* #51; note 245). Subsequently, these two souls appeared in a later generation, Jacob in Rabbi Judah the Prince, the redactor of the Mishnah, and Esau in Antoninos, the Roman ruler. This time, though, they achieved a measure of tikkun, as they were the best of friends, and although they were worlds apart in lifestyle and national allegiance, they related to each other with mutual respect and love (*Reincarnation of Souls* #63).

THE SOUL OF MOSES

The *Zohar* states that the soul of Moses is present in every generation. This is alluded to in the verse we have quoted so many times in this book in relation to reincarnation: "A generation goes and a generation comes but the earth stands forever," where the word "generation" hints to Moses himself. The Arizal explains that the letters of Moses's name in Hebrew – *mem, shin, hei* – are an acronym for *Moshe* (Moses), *Shet* (Seth), and *Hevel* (Abel). As we learned in Chapter One, the very first reincarnation was Seth, who was a gilgul of his murdered brother Abel. Subsequently, all gilgulim stem from this first one. Because Moses was a primary gilgul of the two archetypal figures of Abel and Seth, and as a result of his position as the quintessential leader, his soul returns in every generation in the great sages, mystics, and leaders of Israel.

Even before the emergence of the Jewish people the soul of Moses was present in Noah, the leader of his generation (*Reincarnation of Souls* #116). There are many strong ties between Noah and Moses. Noah was saved from the flood through the safety of an ark and Moses was saved from being drowned like the other Jewish boys by being hidden in an ark. Obviously water also connects these two souls together. The name Moses was given to him by the daughter of Pharaoh when she found him in the reeds of the Nile River, "for I drew him from the water" (Exodus 2:10). In fact, the first letter of Moses is a mem, the same first letter of *mayim*, "water."

The numbers "one hundred twenty" and "forty" further tie Noah and Moses together. Rashi, bringing a midrashic tradition, explains that it took Noah one hundred twenty years to build the ark; Moses lived to the age of one hundred twenty. During the year of the flood, the rains poured down and the waters swelled from below for forty days and forty nights; the number forty appears in Moses' life repeatedly: he was forty when he fled Egypt, herded Jethro's flocks for forty years, and led the Jews through their wanderings in the desert for his last forty years. Dividing Moses' life into three forty-year periods is paralleled by three periods of forty days that he spent on Mount Sinai: first when he initially received the Torah, then when he was pleading for forgiveness for the Jewish people after the grievous sin of the Golden Calf, and again when receiving the second tablets of the law.

Despite the fact that the Torah calls Noah a righteous man, "perfect in his generation," the rabbis were split over the implication of this unusual description. Pointing out that his righteousness was mentioned in relation to his generation, some rabbis asserted that had he lived in a more righteous generation he would have been even greater than he was, while others argued that had he lived, say in the generation of Abraham, he would have been considered quite ordinary (Rashi on Genesis 6:9). What leads the rabbis to have this debate about Noah's character is his lack of leadership. Although he was certainly righteous enough to be chosen by God to save a remnant of humanity, he never attempts to discuss, plead, or argue with God on behalf of his contemporaries to save them from the impending calamity. Additionally, he makes no real attempt to inspire or cajole his generation into changing their ways. The comparison of Noah to Abraham is intentional in that Abraham did plead for the people of Sodom.

To rectify the serious blemish on his soul, Noah is given another opportunity in the person of Moses. After the sin of the Golden Calf Moses pleads with God to forgive the people: "And now if You would forgive their sin – but if not erase me from Your book that You have written" (Exodus 32:32). Even more than the attempt of Abraham to save the people of Sodom, Moses places his very life on the line. With this incredible act of leadership and compassion the soul of Noah receives its tikkun. This is alluded to in the word *mecheni*, "erase me," for when the letters of this word are rearranged they spell *mei noach*, "the waters of

Noah." Additionally, the very same word, "erase," used to describe humanity's destruction in the time of the flood (Genesis 6:7, 7:23), is the word the Torah uses in the above quoted verse.

While Moses was from the soul of Abel, a number of people in his life were from Cain. For example, Moses had to flee Egypt after he killed an Egyptian taskmaster. That Egyptian was of the nefesh of Cain, and in a classic case of "a measure for a measure," Moses buried him in the sand in return for Cain killing Abel and for the earth opening "its mouth" to receive his blood. Cain and Abel, in spite of all that happened, were still brothers and therefore had a deep connection. This is alluded to by the numeric value of "the Egyptian," as he is referred to in the Torah, being equal to the value of the name "Moses." On a deeper, more allegorical, level it can be said that Moses had to kill his Egyptian characteristics in order to assume his true identity as a Jew.

Jethro, Moses' father-in-law, who he held in high esteem, was considered to be the neshama of Cain, his more rectified side. In every soul, especially a soul root, there are positive and negative aspects. The initial letters of the three words Jethro said to Moses, *ani chotencha Yitro*, "I am your father-in-law Jethro," spell *achi*, "my brother." Cain who thought he could escape Divine justice and declared, "Am I my brother's keeper?" received a tikkun through Jethro, who advised Moses on how to set up an orderly and efficient system of judges (*Reincarnation of Souls* #116, note 576).

Korah, the leader of the rebellion against Moses in the desert, embodied the ruach of Cain, as is alluded to in his name which begins with a *kuf*, as does the name Cain, followed by the primary letters of the root for the word ruach, *resh* and *chet*. In another archetypal case of "a measure for a measure," the earth "opened its mouth" to swallow Korah, the same basic expression used to describe how the earth swallowed the blood of Abel when he was killed by Cain.

One of the main figures identified as being a spark of Moses was Rabbi Shimon bar Yochai, a great sage and mystic, who lived in the Land of Israel during the tumultuous period of Roman rule and the overall failure of the Bar Kochba revolt. His teachings and the mystical tradition he handed down were formulated in the *Zohar*, the classic work of Kabbalah, mentioned extensively throughout this book. As Moses received and transmitted the written and oral Torah to Israel, so too Rabbi Shimon, in a period of great persecution, passed on the cumulative mystical tradition to all subsequent generations.

Moses was forced to flee from Egypt, spending forty years in the desert elevating himself spiritually until God appeared to him at the burning bush; Rabbi Shimon bar Yochai, to escape the wrath of the Roman Empire, hid in a cave for thirteen years, during which time he compiled the *Zohar* and worked on perfecting his soul.

The Arizal was also looked upon as possessing a spark of both Moses and Rabbi Shimon. Even when living in Egypt he brought his family to the burial site of Rabbi Shimon in Meron for the first haircut of his three-year-old son. Later when he settled in Safed, he was a frequent visitor to Meron, especially on Lag Ba'omer, the anniversary (*yahrtzeit*) of Rabbi Shimon's death. He celebrated the day with particular fervor and joyous celebration, as Rabbi Shimon had explicitly asked his students not to be sad over his death; instead they should celebrate each year on the date of his passing. The Arizal was especially fond of bringing his students to the burial site of Rabbi Shimon in order to study the *Zohar*. The special ambiance of the place and the spirit of Rabbi Shimon created a unique atmosphere in which to learn. One time when they were gathered at the site, the Arizal described how Rabbi Shimon's inner circle would sit with him when studying together. He showed them the exact spot where Rabbi Shimon and his son, Rabbi Elazar, would sit and where each of the students named in the *Zohar* had their places. He proceeded to reveal to his students how they were the soul sparks of those earlier students of long ago. He then sat in the place of Rabbi Shimon and placed Rabbi Chaim Vital, his primary student, in Rabbi Elazar's place. He then sat each of his students in the place of a particular sage. When they were all seated, he began to expound upon the *Zohar*. He then revealed that the souls of Rabbi Shimon, his students, and many other great sages of the Kabbalistic tradition were present to hear their animated words of Torah. The Arizal noted that while only he was able to envision them, their presence was a true blessing indeed (*Shivchei Ha'ari*, p. 26).

Regarding Moses the Midrash states: "He is the first redeemer and he will be the last redeemer" (*Exodus Rabba* 4:2). This statement ties the souls of Moses and the Mashiach together. The soul connection between Moses and the Mashiach is further evidenced by the first two letters of both – *mem* and *shin* – being identical.

The soul of Moses, as we learned, is present in every generation. Rabbi Shneur Zalman (*Tanya*, chapter 42) explains that every Jew in fact contains a spark of Moses, manifest in the soul's sense of knowing God, a power attributed especially to Moses. This soul power is the aspect of Moses as the first redeemer. As the final redeemer, the spark of Moses in every Jew is manifest in the deep Messianic desire to rectify, redeem, and heal the world (see Yitzchak Ginsburgh, *Rectifying the State of Israel* [Jerusalem: Gal Einai, 2002], p. 152 note 2). This idea from the *Tanya* is based on the slightly earlier teaching of the Ba'al Shem Tov that every Jew possesses a spark of the Mashiach. This holy spark is the innate leadership potential in each individual waiting to become manifest. When enough individuals clarify, harness, and activate their own spark of the Mashiach, a critical mass of redemptive energy will be set in motion, drawing redemption, and ultimately the revelation of the Mashiach, into the world. And parallel to how Moses is the first and last redeemer, he embodies the first reincarnation from Abel to Seth, as well as representing the last gilgulim, when all the souls leave the "body," the treasure house of souls Above, in preparation for the Mashiach.

THE SOUL OF AARON

Haran, Nachor, and Abraham were brothers. Due to Abraham's revolutionary teachings about the One God, and his role in discouraging the prevalent idol worship of the day, he and Haran were brought before Nimrod, who threw Abraham into a fiery furnace when he would not agree to change his ways. A miracle occurred and Abraham emerged unscathed. As he was witnessing the ordeal, Haran decided that if Abraham would come out of the trial safely he too would submit himself to the fire, but if not, he would side with Nimrod. When he saw that Abraham was saved he too offered to be put in the furnace, but this time no miracle occurred and he died. It is explained that since his willingness to be tested was not based on a true belief, he did not merit to be saved.

Haran was reincarnated in Aaron, the first High Priest of Israel, and the brother of Moses. Aaron also had a soul spark of Abraham. The letters of Aaron's name are the same as Haran, with an additional alef at the beginning. Three of the letters in his name also overlap with Abraham's name. Abraham was a gilgul of Adam, who was considered to have worshipped idols (*Sanhedrin* 38b). Abraham was able to rectify that blemish on Adam's soul present within himself through his disavowal of idol worship and his spreading the belief in one God. Significantly, both the names Adam and Abraham begin with an alef (*Likutei Torah, Parshat Ki Tisa; Gate of Reincarnations* 33)

Aaron found himself faced with a situation similar to Haran's in the incident of the Golden Calf. When the people thought that Moses was not returning after being away on Mount Sinai for forty days, they began to look for new leadership (in truth the people had miscalculated the forty days and he actually was not "late" at all). Aaron tried to stall for time in the hope that Moses would return and the people would forget their request for other gods to lead them. His tikkun according to the Arizal would have been accomplished by forcefully resisting the people's desire to craft a golden calf, but after he saw Hur, one of the elders, killed in his own attempt to assuage the people, he reverted to stalling tactics. In desperation he threw all the gold he had collected from the people into the fire, hoping that would be the end of the story; instead, through magical means, a golden calf emerged. It appears the spark of Abraham in Aaron was not enough to prevent him from making the same mistake as Haran had done before him. Hur, according to the Arizal, was a gilgul of Haran's other brother Nachor, who did not have to submit to the same choice as Abraham and Haran when tested by Nimrod. He too had a spark of Adam, but this spark achieved a tikkun, giving him the strength to resist the urge to build and worship an idol.

Despite Aaron's reluctant role in the incident of the Golden Calf he was a very holy and loving soul. Abraham's main quality was loving-kindness and this characteristic permeated Aaron's relations with others. He was beloved by the people as a peacemaker. One of the greatest examples of a leader, peacemaker, and practitioner of loving-kindness, was the great sage Hillel, who was from the same soul spark as Aaron (*Reincarnation of Souls* #116). It is interesting to note that it was Hillel who said: "Be among the students of Aaron, loving peace and pursuing peace, loving people and bringing them closer to the Torah" (*Pirkei Avot* 1:12).

Aaron was never formally punished in his lifetime for his involvement in the fabrication of the Golden Calf, but he was later, when he was subsequently reincarnated in the High Priest Eli. Although a very holy man like Aaron, Eli also showed great weakness in his inability to discipline and control his sons' evil actions. At the end of his forty years as High Priest the Philistines defeated Israel in war and took the Ark of the Covenant. When Eli heard this, he fell backwards from his chair and broke his neck (1 Samuel 4:18). This was considered "a measure for a measure," a punishment for the two tablets of the law being broken due to the sin of the Golden Calf.

Haran later returned as an ibbur into Joshua the High Priest, who is mentioned in the book of the prophet Zecharia: "And he showed me Joshua the High Priest standing before the angel of God, and the adversary standing at his right hand to thwart him. And God said to the adversary, 'God rebukes you, O adversary;

God Who has chosen Jerusalem rebukes you: *for is not this man a brand plucked out of the fire?'* Now Joshua was clothed in filthy garments, and he stood before the angel, who spoke up to those who stood before him, saying, 'Take the filthy garments off him.' And to him he said, 'Behold, I have caused thy iniquity to pass from you; and I clothe you in festive garments'" (Zecharia 3:1–4). God here rewards Haran, for although his entering the fiery furnace was not for the purest of intentions, still there was positive merit in standing up to Nimrod.

We see in these soul histories a number of the dynamics of reincarnation we have studied. First, we see once again the general theme of "a measure for a measure" playing a role in each of these stories. We also see that there are specific sins, e.g., idol worship, needing tikkun. Interestingly enough we also see fire and a certain weakness of character woven throughout, connecting one gilgul to the next. These themes repeat themselves in different guises, and in each life different parts of the soul's attempt to rectify itself are manifest, some being repaired, partially repaired, or not at all.

We also see how the spark of Abraham is expressed in one aspect of Aaron, while the spark of Haran, in a different manner. This is an example of the complex makeup of an individual. Lastly, we observe that great and holy people do not lose all of what they have accomplished because of their mistakes or grievous flaws, instead we see that what needs to be fixed returns to get fixed, and what does not, remains in its properly earned elevated state.

THE SOULS OF NADAB AND ABIHU

Two of the most enigmatic figures in the Torah are Nadab and Abihu, the two sons of Aaron. On the day the Tabernacle was dedicated they tragically died: "The sons of Aaron, Nadab and Abihu, each took his fire pan, they put fire in them, and placed incense upon it, and they brought it before God, a strange fire that He had not commanded them. A fire came forth from before God and consumed them, and they died before God. Moses said to Aaron: Of this did God speak, saying, 'I will be sanctified before those who are nearest Me, thus I will be honored before the entire people'; and Aaron was silent" (Leviticus 10:1–3).

The sages had many interpretations as to what exactly Nadab and Abihu did wrong or what were the factors that led them to act as they did. Among these are that they: drank wine and were drunk at the time of the offering; had not requested permission from Moses; spoke disparagingly of their father and of Moses; and that they were not married, which at their age was considered a very unnatural situation and which the sages attributed to their arrogance in deeming no woman good enough for them. The reason stated simply in the text is that it was an offering not commanded by God and therefore a "strange fire." What makes the incident enigmatic is the end of the above quote – "Of this did God speak, saying, 'I will be sanctified before those who are nearest Me, thus I will be honored before the entire people.'" Moses, according to Rashi, explained to Aaron that he knew the Tabernacle would be sanctified by someone close to God, and he thought it would be Aaron or himself, but now he understood that Nadab and Abihu were greater than the both of them.

As we have said, there are many deep interpretations for why Nadab and Abihu did what they did and why Moses felt that their act made them greater than Aaron and he. This is not the venue for delving into all the profound commentaries regarding this matter. Yet, by looking at the soul histories of Nadab and Abihu, both before and after this incident, many fascinating ideas emerge. According to the Arizal, Nadab was from the ruach of the good side of Cain, and Abihu was from the nefesh and ruach of Cain, and the nefesh of Adam (*Gate of Reincarnations* 33).

According to a simple reading of the text Cain slew Abel after he became angry and jealous that Abel's offering to God had been accepted instead of his (Genesis 4:3–5). We are taught that while it was Cain's idea to bring an offering to God, when the time came to do so, he brought an inferior offering; Abel on the other hand brought the best he had. One could conjecture that on a deep subconscious level Nadab and Abihu's desire to bring an offering on such a holy day was an attempt to rectify their previous mistake of not bringing the best they had.

On another level, their actions were tied to the spirit of tikkun that permeated the dedication of the Tabernacle. In the previous chapter we discussed at length the intentions of Nachshon, the prince of Judah, when he brought his offerings, each one designed to repair a different aspect of history till that time. The Arizal reveals that Nachshon, who was the uncle of Nadab and Abihu, was from the nefesh of Adam, like Abihu. Therefore his name begins with the three letters that spell *nachash*, "snake," whose impurity latches on to the nefesh, the lower soul level of Adam. It is no wonder then that his intention was to fix the damage done by the sin of Adam when he brought the silver bowl (whose numerical value equals 930, the age of Adam) weighing 130 shekels (the number of years Adam spilt seed and his age when Seth was born).

Nadab and Abihu were moved by the same intent of tikkun. Rabbi Ari Kahn explains beautifully how their drinking wine was not an accident; it was rather a deliberate attempt to mend what Adam had torn asunder by eating from the Tree of Knowledge of Good and Evil, which was a grape vine according to an opinion in the Midrash (*Genesis Rabba* 15:7). Noah also attempted to do the same when he planted a vineyard after the flood; however, not only did he fail to mend, his intoxication led to a further tear in the fabric of existence. Nadab and Abihu's coming close to God was further intended to fix the wrong of Adam and Eve when they tried to hide from God (see Ari Kahn, *Explorations* [Southfield, MI: Targum/Feldheim Press, 2001], Parshat Shemini).

Going even deeper, we can understand Nadab and Abihu's offering that day in the context of their father's actions not long before. Aaron had been reticent to stand up to the people during the sin of the Golden Calf. We saw how this was connected to his previous gilgul as Haran, who had also demonstrated indecision regarding idol worship. Both these incidents have a common denominator in fire. And so, on the day of the dedication, Aaron is seen as full of regret for his participation in the Golden Calf incident and remained unsure of being fit to do the service. His lack of confidence was intensified by the fact that the Divine Presence had not yet rested on the Tabernacle, something for which he blamed himself. Moses prayed with him and "a fire went forth from before God and consumed upon the altar the elevation offering and their fats, and the people saw and sang song and fell upon their faces" (see Rashi on Leviticus 9:23–24). Nadab and Abihu wanted to fix not only their own previous incarnation and Adam's sin, but also their father's history of indecision and lack of self-confidence. By bringing an offering on their own initiative they wanted to come close to God in joy and particularly without falling on their faces. Rabbi Kahn points out that in an earlier incident, when God called Moses, Aaron, Nadab, Abihu, and the seventy elders to ascend Mount Sinai before the giving of the Torah they were granted a unique vision of God. Nadab and Abihu responded by eating and drinking and not prostrating themselves (Exodus 24:1–11); they wanted to lead their generation into a new and frontal relationship with God; different from the paradigm they saw currently being practiced.

It is ironic that the Torah records that "Haran died in the lifetime of Terah his father, in his homeland, Ur Kasdim" (Genesis 11:28). Rashi explains that he died in front of (this is the literal translation of the words *al pnei*, which was translated in the quote as "in the lifetime of"), and *because* of his father, as it was Terah who brought his own son before Nimrod to complain about how Abraham had destroyed his idols. Interestingly, Rashi also explains that "Ur Kasdim" means the "fire of Kasdim." Nadab and Abihu, in their attempt to correct their father's indecisiveness by bringing a fire offering, end up also dying before their father. Giving up their lives was in a sense a tikkun for Aaron's inability to do the same at the sin of the Golden Calf and for Haran's lack of commitment when he went into the fire. It is significant to note that their death also came through the agency of fire: "A fire came forth from before God and consumed them, and they died before God."

Although the fire of passion deeply imbedded in the souls of Nadab and Abihu led to their deaths, there was something very positive in their boldness and willingness to give their whole beings. These qualities saved the day in another incident which took place during the forty years in the desert. At the height of a licentious scene when Israel was lured into an orgy by the women of Moab, Zimri, a prince of the tribe of Simon, took Cozbi, a princess of Moab, and publicly challenged Moses. He then took her into his tent, where he had sexual relations with her. The whole scene was so out of control that even Moses and the elders did not know how to react. Phineas, who was an incarnation of Joseph, took the initiative and after respectfully reminding Moses of the correct law, received permission from Moses to act. He took a spear and killed Zimri and Cozbi, thus stopping the plague that had begun to consume the camp. According to the *Zohar*, at the critical moment when Phineas decided to act, the souls of Nadab and Abihu entered him, giving him the strength he needed to step forward alone and kill Zimri and Cozbi, thus averting the people's total destruction. Through his act, Nadab and Abihu were able to rectify their own blemish of not requesting permission before bringing the incense. Further, their pure intention of zealousness in wanting to draw close to God found its correct channel in the zealousness of Phineas, who acted only for the pure motive of wanting to save Israel.

Looking from another angle we see that the weapon that Phineas used was the *romach*, "spear," a word that only appears this one time in the five books of Moses. The numerical value of *romach* is 248, the number of positive *mitzvot* and the number of limbs in the body. From this we learn that Phineas acted with a total sense of being; he was able to channel all his intellectual, emotional, and psychic energies to accomplish this one specific goal. This was only possible due to the *ibbur* of Nadab and Abihu.

Although Nadab and Abihu also acted with a desire to give

themselves totally over to God, yet, as the various teachings tell us, there was a slight hint of arrogance and aloofness in their attitude towards others. They never married, held themselves as special, and spoke out of place before their father and Moses. Though they truly were on a very high level of spirituality, these blemishes acted against them at their fateful moment. Through Phineas they were able to act out of pure motives with no trace of ego involved, thus fixing their own blemish.

Various Kabbalistic traditions state that "Phineas – this is Elijah." It was Elijah who challenged the priests of Ba'al on Mount Carmel through an audacious plan – a plan requiring him to offer a sacrifice outside the confines of the Temple (which ordinarily was prohibited) – that would prove to everyone who was the true God. Each side would construct an altar to their respective deities. Whoever would be able to successfully rain down fire upon their altars would have the proof needed that their god was the true God. Once again fire plays a major role in the story as after a whole day of the priests of Ba'al trying in vain, fire comes from heaven and consumes Elijah's offering. The people respond by enthusiastically recognizing God. The strength, commitment, and zealousness of Nadab, Abihu, and Phineas, shine through Elijah at this climactic event.

Elijah, who ascended to heaven in a fiery chariot, was transformed into an immortal heavenly being. Thus the fire that Nadab and Abihu longed to bring before God came to fruition in the fiery chariot of Elijah. Although the acts of Phineas, Nadab, and Abihu lasted but a few moments, their souls began a process ultimately leading them to immortality. This point is important for educating us in how a single act by an individual can have an impact that is never-ending. Our mystical tradition teaches us that all our actions affect the upper worlds and create energies that may last a lifetime, many generations, or as in Phineas' case, can transform the soul so fundamentally as to give birth to spiritual transcendence. In the Divine realms, past, present, and future are all simultaneous. Similarly, the soul, rooted in God, can, when concentrating and actualizing all its potential, achieve eternity in one act, in a single quintessential moment.

THE SOUL OF RABBI AKIBA

One of the most important and fascinating figures in Jewish history was Rabbi Akiba. Born into a family of converts, he was an illiterate shepherd when Rachel, the daughter of one of the richest men in Israel, fell in love with him. Seeing his great potential she agreed to marry him on condition that he devote himself to the study of Torah. Against her father's wishes they were married and she was promptly disowned. They lived in abject poverty and Rabbi Akiba, after a life-changing experience, fulfilled his promise and went to study Torah. He eventually became the leading sage in Israel and one of the primary transmitters of both the oral and mystical traditions.

According to the Arizal, Rabbi Akiba was an unusual soul in that he possessed both the ruach of Abel and the nefesh of Cain. This combination gave him incredible potential for tikkun and spiritual advancement. As an aside, Hutzpit Hameturgeman, another of the ten martyrs, also included a spark from Cain and Abel. His main spark was from Abel, but it was enclothed in a spark of Cain, much like Jacob, who wore the clothes of Esau, in order to procure the blessing from his father Isaac.

The Arizal further connects the souls of Jacob, Issachar, and Moses to Rabbi Akiba. The letters of Akiba, other than the final letter alef, are the same as Jacob. The name Jacob comes from the root, "heel," for he held on to the heel of his twin brother Esau at birth. According to Kabbalah and Chassidut, Jacob was holding on to the soul of Rabbi Akiba, who was born into a family of converts from the descendants of Esau. Holding on to Esau's heel is reminiscent of Jacob's primordial soul roots coming from Abel, yet very connected to Cain. It also sheds light on the conflicted love-hate association that has characterized the relationship of Jacob and Esau throughout the generations. The Torah states that

Isaac loved Esau because "hunt was in his mouth" (Genesis 25:28). The Arizal taught that Isaac was hunting for holy sparks in the domain of Esau, souls like Rabbi Akiba (*Torah Or* 20c).

Another very deep connection between Jacob and Rabbi Akiba regards the recitation of the Shema, the central statement of faith in the Torah. As Rabbi Akiba was being tortured to death in front of his students by the Romans he told them the time for reciting the morning Shema had arrived. In shock his students asked him how he could focus on the Shema at such a time. He answered them that all his life he longed to fulfill the commandment to love God with all your soul, an idea contained in the verse recited immediately after the Shema. Now that he had the opportunity to fulfill that longing should he not grasp it? With his last breath he said the Shema, the reverberations of which have echoed through the generations. In our times, millions of Jews went to the gas chambers with the Shema on their lips.

Although the Shema is only recorded later in the book of Deuteronomy, its recitation arises, according to the Midrash, at two significant moments in Jacob's life. When Joseph and Jacob reunite after twenty-two years, Joseph falls on his father's neck and cries. The Torah, interestingly enough, does not record Jacob's reaction. Rashi brings the tradition that at that climactic moment Jacob was reciting the Shema, his expression of gratitude upon seeing his long lost son, and his acknowledgment of God's plan coming to fruition. Later, on his death bed, Jacob gathered his sons in order to reveal what would happen to them at the end of days. At that moment God's presence left him. Jacob worried that it was because his sons were not worthy. When they saw their father's consternation they all intuitively said the Shema together, in order to assure him that his life's mission to establish the foundation of a holy nation was not in vain.

As we have learned, the spark of Moses returns in the leaders of each generation. Rabbi Akiba was one of the most important links in the transmission of the Torah given to Moses at Mount

Sinai. Like Moses who lived to be one hundred twenty years old, so did Rabbi Akiba.

Another beautiful connection between these two souls is found in the inspiring story of how Rabbi Akiba came to the study of Torah. Despite his promise to his wife, his initial attempts at learning were totally unsuccessful. Discouraged and embarrassed, he was on the verge of giving up when one day while sitting by a spring he noticed how a steady drip of water had made an indentation in the rock. In an epiphany he realized that if water, which is soft, could carve out something as hard as rock, certainly words of Torah that are compared to water could penetrate his mind and heart. With that inspiration he returned to his studies. From being saved in a basket on the Nile River, to meeting his wife at the well, to not being allowed into the Land of Israel because to bring forth water he hit the rock instead of speaking to it, water played a crucial role in Moses' life as well. His name Moses, was given to him by the daughter of Pharaoh "…for I drew him from the water" (Exodus 2:10).

The tribe of Issachar was known to include many wise sages. In the book of 1 Chronicles (12:33) it states that this tribe "…knew the understanding of times to know what Israel should do, their heads were two hundred, and their brothers went according to [the word of] their mouth." The Midrash explains that these two hundred were heads of the Sanhedrin and their understanding of the times relates to their particular wisdom in knowing how to calculate the Hebrew calendar (*Genesis Rabba* 72:5, 98:12). Rabbi Akiba was certainly among the wisest of Israel.

It is interesting to note that Issachar was born to Leah after she traded mandrakes, considered an aphrodisiac, with Rachel, who was jealous of her sister, who had given birth to many sons, whereas she had still not given birth (Genesis 30:14–17). This reminds us of the jealousy Cain felt for Abel after they brought an offering to God. While the sisters were able to resolve their differences peacefully, the jealousy of Cain for Abel resulted in murder. The birth of Issachar can be seen to be a fixing for those raw emotions; and his presence in Rabbi Akiba was perhaps a mediating balance between the souls of Cain and Abel within him.

The Arizal further connected Rabbi Akiba and his second wife with being the rectification of two previous couples: Shechem and Dinah, and Zimri and Cozbi. In response to Shechem raping Dinah and holding her hostage, Simon and Levi took revenge and killed the men of the city of Shechem. This occurred after the sons of Jacob had told Shechem that he would be able to marry Dinah if everyone in the town would circumcise themselves, which they did. Although Shechem did rape Dinah, the Torah states that he became deeply attached to her and spoke to her heart, implying some sort of soul attachment, albeit in a very un-rectified manner. These two souls returned in Zimri and Cozbi who were once again brought together in very desire-driven circumstances, as explained earlier. A spark of Zimri, returned in Rabbi Akiba and Cozbi received her repair through Rabbi Akiba's second wife, who at one time had been a high society Roman matron, the wife of Turnusrufus (*Reincarnation of Souls # 76*).

According to tradition, Rome comes from the lineage of Esau. The fact that Rabbi Akiba married a converted Roman woman ties in with his carrying a spark of Jacob. It also reflects on his having within himself sparks of both Cain and Abel, and from his being from a family of converts from the lineage of Esau. The love-hate relationship between Jacob and Esau, and as manifest in Cain and Abel, is reflected in Rabbi Akiba leading a revolt against Rome on the one hand and marrying a Roman convert on the other. There are scores of stories in the Talmud recording the hatred Rome had for the Jews, as well as their very strong fascination and respect for Jewish wisdom.

Another connection between these three couples is seen in the number "24,000." Rabbi Akiba had 24,000 students, all of whom died during the time of the Bar Kochba revolt against

Rome. According to the Arizal, these 24,000 students were the incarnation of the 24,000 people who died in the plague that had broken out in the camp during the incident surrounding Zimri and Cozbi. It is further taught that 24,000 was also the number of men killed in Shechem, who later incarnated into those who were killed at the time of Zimri (*Emek Hamelech* 40b). The fact that the men of Shechem circumcised themselves was considered a merit, thus their return in the souls of Jews. Yet their tikkun was far from complete. Later they returned as students of Torah, certainly a great improvement, but once again they fell short, as tradition teaches that they died due to their inability to show honor and respect to each other.

After the 24,000 students of Rabbi Akiba died he trained five students. Among them were Rabbi Shimon bar Yochai and Rabbi Meir. It is interesting to note that the first letters of the names of these three figures, each one great in their own right, spell the word shema. In the Torah the last letter of shema, an ayin, is written large. The name Akiba begins with an ayin, and its being large alludes to the fact that he was the teacher of the other two (see Yitzchak Ginsburgh, *Rectifying the State of Israel* [Jerusalem: Gal Einai, 2002], pp. 17–20 and footnote 25).

The souls of Rabbi Akiba and Rabbi Shimon were thus connected in many ways. On Lag Ba'omer, the 33rd day of the counting of the *omer*, the fifty-day period between Pesach and Shavuot, two events are commemorated. The first is the cessation of the plague that killed the students of Rabbi Akiba and the second is the death of Rabbi Shimon. It was Rabbi Akiba, alone among his colleagues, who entered the *Pardes* – a deep level of mystical meditation – in peace, and came out in peace. The mystical tradition that Rabbi Akiba transmitted was passed down to Rabbi Shimon and ultimately revealed in the *Zohar*.

A widespread custom of Lag Ba'omer is the bonfire. The fires of Lag Ba'omer represent the light of the inner dimension of the Torah, the spiritual, mystical Jewish tradition handed down to our own day. This light represents the deepest longing of the soul to be close to God and to understand the depths of the Torah. Rabbi Akiba was tortured by having his skin scraped off by burning rakes. He took that fire and transformed it by sacrificing his life with a fiery love of God. At the moment Rabbi Akiba transformed the burning combs of hatred and torture into a fiery determination and love of God it was transferred to his student, Rabbi Shimon. He too was persecuted by the Roman authorities, but managed to escape to a secluded cave where he hid for twelve years. During those years the fire of Torah burned bright as he wrote the *Zohar*. His fire for Torah, received from Rabbi Akiba, was transmuted into understanding the light of the inner dimensions of Torah. After twelve years, Rabbi Shimon was informed by Heaven that he could leave the cave. According to the Talmud, upon seeing a farmer working his fields, a fire burst forth from him and "burnt up" the farmer, for he could not comprehend someone pursuing the mundane instead of the brilliant light of Torah. In response, God ordered him back to the cave until he could temper his passion, until he could use his own fire in a more productive way (*Shabbat* 33b). Upon leaving the cave a year later, Rabbi Shimon once again gathered his students around him and passed this holy fire on to them. On his death bed he assured his distressed students that they should rejoice and not be saddened. The eternal flame of Torah passed on to him by his teacher, Rabbi Akiba, in his recitation of the Shema, was now transmitted through his eternal teachings to them.

It is described that a great light filled the room at the time of Rabbi Shimon's death. That light has been handed down from generation to generation and is symbolized in the bonfire of Lag Ba'omer. The law of conservation of energy applies to the spiritual as well as the physical world. Spiritual longing and light is never destroyed, it is always transformed and passed on. It will be this light that will ultimately reveal itself in the final redemption, when Israel will become "a light unto the nations" (see Avraham Arieh Trugman, *Seeds and Sparks* [Southfield, MI: Targum Press, 2003], pp 199–202)

We mentioned above that Rabbi Shimon bar Yochai was from the same soul spark as Moses, as was Rabbi Akiba. The significance of this will be realized after contemplating yet another connection between Moses and Rabbi Akiba. In an amazing Talmudic passage, Moses' ascent to heaven is described. As he comes into the heavenly realms, he finds God putting crowns on the Hebrew letters. Moses inquires as to what God is doing, to which God responds that in the future someone named Akiba ben Joseph will derive mounds of laws from these crowns. Moses asks to see this person and he is transported to the future, where he finds himself in the back of Rabbi Akiba's study hall. To Moses' chagrin he is unable to follow Rabbi Akiba's brilliant dissertation. He only finds comfort when Rabbi Akiba states that what he has just taught was transmitted by Moses from Sinai. He then says to God: You have such a person and you give the Torah through me? God responds enigmatically: Be quiet – this is the way it has been determined by Me. Moses then asks: What will his reward be for being such a Torah luminary? He turns around and is granted a vision of Rabbi Akiba being tortured to death. In shock Moses exclaims: This is Torah and this is its reward? To which God answers: Be quiet – this is the way it has been determined by Me (*Menachot* 29b).

Rebbe Nachman of Breslov explained that the idiom, "Be quiet – this is the way it has been determined by Me," when understood more literally yields a much different meaning than a seemingly sharp rebuke. When translated more literally this expression reads: Be quiet – this is how it is elevated in thought before Me. According to Rebbe Nachman, the entire phrase can be understood as God telling Moses, when you are quiet and enter a deep state of meditation and contemplation, this is how you elevate yourself in thought so that you will be able to grasp the profound meaning of what I am showing you.

Although a spark of Moses was present in Rabbi Akiba, Rabbi Shimon was from the very same soul spark and therefore an even more primary manifestation. In the Talmudic story, Rabbi Akiba acknowledged his learning came from Moses, while Moses was truly humbled in the presence of Rabbi Akiba. In the future, the soul spark of Moses, strongly manifest in Rabbi Shimon, actually became one of the primary students of Rabbi Akiba, especially in the transmission of the mystical tradition!

THE SOUL OF THE BA'AL SHEM TOV

The Ba'al Shem Tov, the founder of the Chassidic movement, was one of the most influential figures in recent Jewish history. Despite the fact that he did not personally record his teachings, and in his lifetime he had a relatively small number of students, his influence profoundly affected not only those who joined the Chassidic ranks, but all of Jewish thought. Within Chassidic teachings there are a number of ideas as to which souls were reincarnated in the Ba'al Shem Tov. Rabbi Yitzchak Ginsburgh brings these ideas together and teaches that he was a combination of four souls, one new soul and three old souls. When new and old souls come together it is the new soul that occupies the more inner dimension of the individual, while the older souls occupy the more exterior aspects. As discussed above, new souls do not descend all that often, but when they do they usually have a major impact on the world. The new soul of the Ba'al Shem Tov manifested itself in the original and revolutionary tone of his teachings and his natural charisma.

The first of the old souls within the Ba'al Shem Tov was the soul of a hidden tzaddik who lived in Safed around the time of the Arizal. His level of holiness, learning, and character development was so hidden no one recognized what an exalted spiritual level he was on. Once, Elijah the Prophet was sent from on High to test if his modesty was truly that special. In the course of conversation, Elijah asked him what he did on his bar mitzvah day. Somewhat embarrassed, the hidden tzaddik would not reveal anything other than to say that whatever he did, it was all for the sake of Heaven. Due to his true and sincere humbleness it was decreed that Elijah would come and teach him. Despite his being worthy of learning with Elijah, he remained completely hidden during his life. Due to this he merited to incarnate into the Ba'al Shem Tov, who despite his tremendous influence was hidden for much of his life, and even after revealing himself, remained very humble and low-key in displaying his tremendous soul powers.

The second old soul ironically was none other than Rabbi Sa'adya Gaon, who was presented in the first chapter as one of the primary opponents to the teachings of reincarnation. We clarified that he objected to a belief in reincarnation of one soul continually transmigrating from one body to the next, and not like the teachings of the Arizal, which are far more complex and in fact agree with Rabbi Sa'adya on this point. As mentioned above, the Ba'al Shem Tov was instrumental in popularizing the Arizal's teachings on gilgul, bringing it into the mainstream of Jewish thought.

Rabbi Sa'adya used to relate the following about how he had learnt that teshuva is truly an ongoing process. Once he came to a town and was hosted by a very nice but simple man who did not know his identity. When Rabbi Sa'adya left town he bid farewell and thanked the man for his gracious hospitality. Soon after, the man learned that he had hosted the great scholar, Rabbi Sa'adya. He ran after him and begged forgiveness for not having treated him better. Rabbi Sa'adya assured him that his hospitality had been impeccable and that he had nothing to regret. The man, still feeling terrible, said, "But had I known who you are, I would have treated you so much better." Rabbi Sa'adya immediately learned from the man's sincere declaration a profound lesson for life, which he then applied to a person's relationship with God. He taught that if a person is to grow spiritually each day he must not be frozen or handicapped by yesterday's concept of God. If he would have known yesterday what he knows about God today, he would have loved and served Him that much more then! Similarly, the Ba'al Shem Tov emphasized a service of God based on a constant process of self-improvement and of serving God anew everyday. It was in fact a very fundamental component of his teachings.

According to Chassidic tradition, the last component in the soul constellation of the Ba'al Shem Tov was that of King David. This accounts for the Messianic thrust of the Chassidic movement, as originally taught by the Ba'al Shem Tov. He urged a more proactive and energetic participation in the process leading to the Messianic era. Earlier we discussed how the Arizal revealed that he had been given permission to reveal what was previously hidden due to a fundamental change occurring in all the worlds, and as a result of the lights that were beginning to shine illuminating the way for Mashiach. The teachings of the inner dimensions of Torah were instrumental in this process and the Ba'al Shem Tov, more than any other person, popularized the teachings of Kabbalah, and created an entire movement based on its principles. Like King David, the Ba'al Shem Tov feared no person, his fear and awe was of God alone. And like King David, the sweet singer of Israel, the Ba'al Shem Tov brought song and joy from the shadow of exile and placed it at the center of a Jew's service to God.

It is told that the Ba'al Shem Tov desired to come to Israel in order to meet the Ohr Hachaim, a great teacher who had just moved to the Land of Israel from Morocco. He felt that if they could come together it would hasten the coming of Mashiach. The Ba'al Shem Tov was considered to be the nefesh of David, whereas the Or Hachaim contained David's ruach. Setting out on the journey towards Israel, he actually made it as far as Istanbul, but was thwarted in the final leg of the journey. His attempt to come to Israel was living testimony to his belief that a new age was dawning. Although he did not physically make it to Israel, his endeavors inspired many of his followers to move to Israel, paving the way for the steady and miraculous ingathering of the exiles that continues unabated in our own day.

CONCLUDING THOUGHTS

It is written in the Talmud: "Everything follows the conclusion" (*Berachot* 12a). In our context that means pondering the following question: After all we have learned regarding gilgul, what can we walk away with, what ideas can we positively integrate into our lives? Since each person is different and views the world in his or her own unique manner, this is not a simple question to answer. Inasmuch as I began writing this book looking for answers to real circumstances in my life, perhaps the most honest way to conclude is to share what I personally learned from the material I studied and attempted to impart to the reader, and hope it rings true for you as well.

As I dove into the various texts regarding gilgul, especially the teachings of the Arizal, I was struck by how profound life is and how the true picture of the whole universe is vastly different from our initial, superficial understanding of life's experiences. As I contemplated how everything physical and spiritual enclothed ever deeper layers of reality, it forced me to look closer into every aspect of life. I have slowly come to realize that if I want to understand the true context of my existence, I need to greatly expand my consciousness. Each level of expansion brings a wider realm of existence into focus, opening new and greater vistas.

These realizations ultimately lead me to the multidimensional matrix explained at the end of Chapter Four. I even dreamed about it. In my dream, I found myself in a transparent and translucent cube, floating somewhere in open space. I became aware that past, present, and future were flowing through the enclosed space, and all the various parts of my soul as they had become manifest in different lifetimes were present in the cube as well. Then I became aware that there were multiple dimensions seen and not seen all around me and even within me. In essence, everything in the universe was existent in the cube. Everything in the cubed matrix was simultaneous and accessible. Despite all this I was not actually able to grasp any particular idea, fact, or memory, rather I was awestruck and content with the realization that the matrix is as real as anything I had ever known. And then I awoke. There was something very primordial, yet at the same time futuristic, about the experience, and it has come to represent all I have learned about – not just the dynamics of gilgul, but perhaps even more important, the overall context and ramification of these teachings.

On a very practical level I was inspired by the meaning and immediacy of man rectifying himself and his world, and the importance of making the most of life. Although there exists the danger of becoming complacent, knowing that if you don't get it right this time you will have more chances, for me it had the opposite effect. When I contemplate how many levels there are to the soul and how much closer each rectified soul level brings us to God, I am more motivated to get on with the task of assuming my birthright as a true and consummate image of God.

I was also fascinated with the process of "connecting the dots" of the Torah and of life. Each additional connection we make somehow strengthens the entire fabric of existence in ways we cannot really grasp, yet we can feel the surge of spiritual energy running through the mind and heart. The web of relationships, associations, and connections that bind reality together, whether in regard to gilgul, nature, history, the Jewish people, all humanity, the entire universe, and all the spiritual worlds, ultimately brings us to the realization that all is one and all is from God.

A question is often asked: Does God still speak to man? And if yes, why do we not hear Him? God does still speak to us, but now it is through the circumstances of our lives. When we realize that, we become aware that God is talking to us loud and clear. The hints to our previous lives are all around us, as are those things we need to fix in order to move on. We need to learn to interpret the circumstances of our lives, as with a dream, extracting the symbolic lessons being offered us.

In particular, the teachings of gilgul and their overarching connection to how God dispenses justice in the world answers for me some of the most perplexing and vexing questions about life. Although many occurrences in my personal life and the world around me are still an enigma, my faith in God's goodness and fairness have been strengthened. Just knowing that there is a reason for everything, that it is ultimately for the good, and that there is a just and true accounting, allows me to more easily accept those situations in life beyond my ability to understand.

The advice and position of the Ba'al Shem Tov that knowing the details of previous lives is not all that critical, whereas the constant work of self-improvement and spiritual advancement in the here and now is what is important, seems to me a healthy and balanced one. Despite nearly eighteen months of being engrossed with this subject I have not once considered undergoing hypnosis or some other method in an attempt to unearth previous lifetimes. Frankly, I am too wary of the results not being the real thing. I am content with using prayer and meditation to contact deeper levels of soul and the insight they afford for understanding who I am, where I am coming from, and where I am going.

For this reason the question of the Ba'al Shem Tov – what do you remember? – resonates deeply within my soul. The exercise of peering intensely into the inner dimensions of the soul is certainly an exciting and challenging opportunity. My intuition tells me that, with the proper efforts, awesome realizations await anyone sincerely interested in discovering these new horizons. For deep within the soul lies each person's own matrix, the collective unconscious of one's particular soul root, as well as its connection to the Jewish people, all humanity, and the entire universe.

There is a custom to stand for the evening Kiddush, the liturgical declaration that declares the sanctity of Shabbat. One explanation for this custom is that reciting and hearing Kiddush is reminiscent of taking the witness stand, for we are testifying that God created the heavens and earth and rested on the seventh day, and to give testimony we must stand. The question could be asked: How can someone give testimony for something he did not actually witness? The answer is that on some deep level we were there!! The soul as an actual part of God was, as it were, still within the very essence of God, and in some primordial level of memory can still remember being at the initial moment of creation. This is similar to a fetus being taught the entire Torah in the womb. Even though it forgets, it is always there, always ready to be re-accessed.

Another area that intrigues me and has inspired me to start thinking in a new way revolves around understanding the real complexity of who "I" am. It is so much more multifaceted than I ever imagined, and I find it does not intimidate me at all to think of myself as a combination of souls that may change from one lifetime to another, and even within this life. I especially relate to gilgul bachayim, "reincarnation in [one] life," as I have personally experienced it, but never had a name for it. The awareness that our individual souls are part of larger and larger soul sparks and roots is strangely comforting. It gives a new appreciation of belonging to something greater than our rather narrow self-definition. This is especially true in relation to the Jewish people. The feeling of destiny and purpose, particularly in the tremendous times in which we live, is sometimes overwhelming, yet reassuring as well.

The teachings of Judaism, and of the Arizal in particular, are infused with purpose and intention. Everyone and everything counts, no one is expendable, and every thought, word, and action has infinite potential. Nothing is forgotten, everything is judged, and God's goodness and fairness ultimately win the day. Although the burden of living in an un-rectified, and at times very broken world, is occasionally almost too much to bear, the fact that God has done this purposely in order to give the human free choice and a chance to partner with Him in completing creation, is both a responsibility and a great privilege. May we be up to the challenge and live life to its full potential, rising from strength to strength, till each person fulfills his or her purpose and the world merits its final redemption.

GLOSSARY

Arizal – Rabbi Isaac Luria (1534–1572); Arizal is an acronym for Ha'eloki **R**abbenu **I**saac **Z**ichrono **L**ivracha, "The Godly Rabbi Isaac of blessed memory," as well as, **A**shkenazi **R**abbi **I**saac (his father was called Luria Ashkenazi). He was born in Jerusalem, but after the death of his father when he was only five years old, his family moved to Egypt where his uncle provided for the family. After mastering the written and oral tradition at a very early age he delved into Kabbalah and studied in semi isolation in a shack along the Nile River for many years, till going to Safed in 1570. In the less than three years he spent in Safed his teachings revolutionized the study of Kabbalah and all subsequent study of the subject is founded on his teachings up to our day.

Atbash – a Kabbalistic alphabet in which the first letter of the alphabet (alef) is exchanged for the last letter (tav), the second letter (bet) for the second last letter (shin), and so forth.

Ba'al Shem Tov – "Master of the Good Name [of God];" the name by which Rabbi Israel ben Eliezer (1698–1760), the founder of the Chassidic movement was known.

Chafetz Chaim – Rabbi Israel Meir Hacohen Kagan (1838–1933). His classic work, for which he was nicknamed, *Chafetz Chaim*, is a compilation of the laws regarding the misuse of speech. He is also the author of the *Mishnah Berurah*, a legal commentary

181

on the laws of daily life as presented in the *Shulchan Aruch Orach Chaim.*

Chassidut – teachings of the Chassidic movement.

Chaya – "living one"; the fourth ascending level of soul, associated with the higher aspect of the superconscious.

Chessed – "loving-kindness" and "mercy"; one of the ten sefirot, it is the first of the seven lower "emotive" sefirot.

Elokim – one of the names of God, it is associated with nature and the laws that rule the natural world. It also denotes God's attributes of judgment and power.

Gehenom – "hell" or "purgatory."

Gematria – "numerology"; the Kabbalistic method of comparing and analyzing numerical equivalencies between words in order to find deeper layers of meaning.

Gevurah – "power" or "strength"; one of the ten sefirot; also associated with God's name Elokim and the attribute of fear/ awe.

Gilgul – "reincarnation."

Gilgul bachayim – "reincarnation in life"; a concept wherein a person is so completely transformed it is as if he or she was a new incarnation in the same body and life.

Hashem – "the Name [of God]"; refers to the four-letter Name of God, which due to it not being pronounced the way it is written, is simply referred to as "Hashem."

Hitlabeshut – "enclothment"; one of the major themes running through the teachings of the Arizal, it describes how entities are enclothed within other entities.

Ibbur – "impregnation"; the term used by the Arizal to explain how a departed soul may enter a body in this world for a limited time in order to either assist that body's soul achieve rectification or in an effort to assist itself.

Kabbalah – the root of the word means "receiving" and is also used to denote a tradition which has been passed down through the generations; the mystical or esoteric teachings of the Torah.

Kaddish – the mourner's prayer traditionally recited for eleven (or twelve) months after the death of one of seven close relatives (father, mother, son, daughter, brother, sister, or spouse).

Keter – "crown"; the first and highest of the ten sefirot; associated with the superconscious levels of the soul, especially faith, divine pleasure, and will.

Kohanim – "priests"; descendents of Aaron the first High Priest who was from the tribe of Levi. The Kohanim performed the main service in the Temple.

Levi'im – "Levites"; descendants of the tribe of Levi who had special duties in the Temple service, especially of playing music and singing.

Mashiach – "anointed one"; the Hebrew term for the Messiah, the future redeemer from the line of King David and about whom all the prophets prophesied. The Messianic era will be one of universal peace and brotherhood, when "the knowledge of God will cover the earth like the waters cover the seabed" (Isaiah 11:9).

Maimonides – Rabbi Moses ben Maimon, known by the acronym Rambam (1135–1204); one of the greatest legalists and thinkers of the last millennium, his codification of Jewish law in the *Mishneh Torah* is a foundation of all Jewish law and practice; also the author of the *Guide to the Perplexed*.

Mazal – from the root word meaning "to flow"; a spiritual channel or conduit of Divine beneficence; the term used for the constellations.

Midrash – an important component of the oral Torah, written chiefly in Israel between the second and eighth centuries, it consists of homiletic teachings of the Bible. Some of the better known collections include: The *Rabbah* series on the five books of Moses (i.e., *Genesis Rabba*, *Exodus Rabba*, etc...), *Midrash Tanchuma*, *Pirkei Derabbi Eliezer*, *Tanna Devei Eliyahu* and *Midrash Tehillim*. Other collections focusing more on legalistic subjects include the *Mechilta*, *Sifra*, and *Sifrei*.

Mishnah – compiled by Rabbi Judah the Prince in approximately 200 CE, it organized for the first time the oral Torah in written form. Comprising six orders, the Mishnah till this day forms the basis of the oral law.

Mishneh Torah – see Maimonides.

Mitzvah – "commandment" or law. There are 613 mitzvot (pl. of mitzvah) in the five books of Moses; 248 positive and 365 prohibitive. In a wider sense the term also includes rabbinic laws and is also used to refer to good deeds.

Nachmanides – Rabbi Moses ben Nachman (1194–1270) is known by the acronym Ramban; a great scholar and important link in the transmission of the Kabbalistic tradition. In 1263 he valiantly defended Judaism in front of the king and representatives of the Catholic Church. Although he won the debate, or perhaps because he won it, he had to flee the country. He came to the Land of Israel in 1267 and lived there till his death a few years later.

Nazir – refers to a person who would take an oath to refrain from eating or drinking any product from the grape and also from cutting his or her hair for a period of time. The source for this mitzvah appears in the book of Numbers (6:1–21).

Nefesh – "creature" or "soul"; more specifically, it relates to the lowest of the five levels of soul, sometimes referred to as the "animal soul," associated with the instinctive or behavioral aspect of soul.

Neshama – "soul"; the third ascending level of soul, associated with the intellect.

Nisan – the Hebrew name for the first month of the year during which Pesach, Passover, is celebrated; associated with redemption, freedom, and renewal.

Olam hatikkun – "the world of rectification"; the name the Arizal used to refer to the present state of reality, whose motivating purpose is to repair the damage from the "breaking of the vessels."

Partzuf – "profile"; pl. partzufim; a constellation of sefirot; represents a further development of individual sefirot that allows them to interact with each other in dynamic ways.

Pirkei Avot – "Ethics of the Fathers"; one of the sixty-three tractates of the Mishnah and one of the most important compilations of sayings of the sages, especially in the area of morals and ethics.

Rabbi Menachem Mendel Schneersohn – the dynamic seventh leader of the Chabad movement; during his over forty-year reign he established over 1,000 Jewish institutions in virtually every corner of the globe and wrote prolifically.

Rabbi Shneur Zalman of Liady – (1745–1812) was the founder of the Chabad Chassidic movement and author of the *Tanya* and *Shulchan Aruch Harav*. He was a student of the Maggid of Mezerich. Due to his attempts to mediate between the new Chassidic movement and other Jewish groups he was arrested by the Russian authorities. He was released and continued to teach and write until his death when fleeing Napoleon's advancing army.

Rabbi Yitzchak Ginsburgh – one of the greatest living teachers of Kabbalah and Chassidut, he has authored over sixty books on a wide range of subjects. Many of his books synthesize Torah and Kabbalah wisdom with the secular sciences and arts.

Rashi – Rabbi Shlomo Yitzchaki (1040–1105), known by the acronym Rashi. He lived in France and was one of the most important and prolific commentators of the last thousand years. His commentary on the Bible and Talmud are still studied and are universally admired.

Rebbe Nachman – the great grandson of the Ba'al Shem Tov (1772–1811); the author of the Chassidic classic *Likutei Moharan* and teller of many of the most famous of the Chassidic allegorical stories for which the movement is known. He is buried in Uman, Ukraine; every year on Rosh Hashana tens of thousands of his followers gather to be near his grave.

Ruach – "spirit"; the second ascending level of soul, associated with the emotions.

Ruach hakodesh – Divine inspiration (literally "holy spirit"); an inspired state of consciousness.

Safed – (Hebrew, *Tzfat*); one of the four "holy cities" of Israel, along with Jerusalem, Hebron, and Tiberias. Situated in the high mountains of the Galilee, Safed has a special mystical ambience that has drawn scholars and mystics throughout the ages. Especially in the 1500's it became a magnet for Jewish mystics and is most known for the great Kabbalists who lived and taught there, including the Arizal.

Sanhedrin – the Jewish High Court of 71 ordained scholars played a very important role in the life of ancient Israel. They convened in one of the chambers of the Temple in Jerusalem. After the Temple's destruction it moved from place to place till its disbandment in the 4th century CE.

Sefirot – pl. of sefira; a conduit of Divine energy or life force. The model of the ten sefirot is one of the primary paradigms used in Kabbalah to describe the interface between God and the spiritual and physical worlds, as well as the construct of the human soul.

Seven Noachide laws – according to the Torah there are seven universal laws incumbent on all humanity from the time of Noah and for all time. These include the general prohibitions of worshiping any entity other than the One God, blasphemy, murder, theft, adultery, and eating the flesh of a live animal. In addition, there is the positive commandment to establish courts of law to ensure the creation of a just society.

Shalem vachetzi – "a whole and a half"; a concept developed by Rabbi Abraham Abulafia, a 13th century Kabbalist, pays note to the numerical ratio of a whole number and its half, when applied to the numerical equivalent of words and their associated concepts.

Shechina – "indwelling"; this term is associated with the "feminine" aspect of Divinity and the immanent presence of God in the world.

Shem Mishmuel – Rabbi Shmuel Bornstein (1856–1920); *Shem Mishmuel* is the name of his extensive commentary on the five books of Moses and the holidays. He was the son of Rabbi Abraham Bornstein, known as the Sochatchover Rebbe, a leading figure in the Chassidic movement and great scholar.

Shema – considered by many as the most basic statement of faith of Judaism: "Hear (i.e., understand), O Israel, Hashem is our God [Elokim], Hashem is one" (Deuteronomy 6:4).

Slonimer Rebbe – Rabbi Sholom Noach Berezovsky; until his recent death he was the leader of the Slonim Chassidic community in Jerusalem; author of *Netivot Shalom*, a very popular commentary on the five books of Moses, the holidays, and character development.

Talmud – literally means "learning"; it is comprised of the Mishnah (see above) and the Gemara, the extensive discussions of the sages as they clarified the Mishnah. Along with the better known Babylonian Talmud codified in the 6th century, there is also the Jerusalem Talmud completed in the 3rd century.

Tanya – the classic work written by Rabbi Shneur Zalman of Liady (see entry). *Tanya* is also known as *Likutei Amarim* and *Sefer shel Beinonim*.

Tashlich – a ritual performed on Rosh Hashana, the Jewish New Year, when participants throw breadcrumbs, symbolically representing sins, into a body of water, preferably a flowing stream or river with fish.

Techiyat Hameitim – the "resurrection of the dead," the last of the thirteen principles of faith formulated by Maimonides is the resurrection of the dead. Ezekiel prophesied regarding this future event, which according to tradition will occur after the coming of the Mashiach.

Teshuva – "repentance" or more literally, returning to God. The ten days between Rosh Hashana and Yom Kippur, when Jews make a practical and spiritual accounting, are referred to as the Ten Days of Teshuva.

Tikkun – "rectification" and "repair."

Tikkunei Zohar – "Rectifications of the Zohar"; one of the important components of Zoharic literature attributed to Rabbi Shimon bar Yochai.

Tishrei – the Hebrew name for the seventh month of the year; the holidays of Rosh Hashana, Yom Kippur, Succot, and Shemini Atzeret take place during this month.

Tohu – "chaos"; the world of chaos (olam hatohu) manifests the primordial state of un-rectified reality, when the initial, premature vessels of Creation could not contain the powerful lights of Creation, causing the "breaking of the vessels."

Tzaddik – "righteous individual"; pl. tzaddikim.

Yahrtzeit – the Yiddish term for commemoration of the anniversary of a person's death. The day is usually marked by saying Kaddish, the mourner's prayer, lighting candles, giving charity, and learning Torah, all done in the merit of the departed soul.

Yechida – "single [unique] one"; the highest of the five levels of soul, associated with the Divine aspect of soul.

Zohar – "brilliance"; one of the most fundamental and important texts of Kabbalah; the basic mystical teachings taught by Rabbi Shimon bar Yochai to his students and handed down through the generations till they were compiled, edited, and publicized in the early 1200's in Spain.

ABOUT THE AUTHOR

Rabbi Avraham Arieh Trugman has been involved in Jewish education for over thirty years. As a founding member of Moshav Meor Modiim in 1976, he went on to be the director of the Moshav's Center of Jewish Education, which successfully ran annual programs for over five thousand participants from twenty-five countries. In 1988 he took the position of regional director of NCSY in Denver, Colorado, where he and his wife created a new region. He returned to Israel in 1995 and currently serves as the director of Ohr Chadash: New Horizons in Jewish Experience, which he founded with his wife.

Rabbi Trugman is the author of *Seeds and Sparks: Inspiration and Self-Expression through the Cycles of Jewish Life* (Targum Press, 2003), *The Mystical Power of Music* (Targum Press, 2005), *The Mystical Meaning of Dreams* (Targum Press, 2006), and *The Mystical Nature of Light: Divine Paradox of Creation* (Devorah Publishing Company, 2008). He appears at Shabbat programs and lectures extensively worldwide.

OHR CHADASH

New Horizons in Jewish Experience

Ohr Chadash is a non-profit education organization serving English-speaking students enrolled at various universities, yeshivot, seminaries, and long-term programs in Israel, as well as adults, immigrants, and native Israelis. We provide a wide range of programs in an open, joyous, non-coercive, and spiritual atmosphere, where participants are able to explore Judaism at their own pace. Programs include classes, workshops, lunch-and-learn, concerts, Shabbatons, home hospitality, leadership training, seminars, tours, counseling, and social action projects. We combine heart and mind and cater to each participant's special needs. We provide a home away from home for students and visitors and maintain strong relationships for years to come.

Ohr Chadash has run and participated in programs for tens of thousands of people from the full gamut of Jewish backgrounds. With the inspiration and skills that students gain they return to their home communities eager to take leadership roles. Many students and adults return to Israel and the bonds become even stronger. Through our extensive website and e-mail we maintain communication with thousands of alumni and have managed to build a real extended family feeling. As educational follow-up, Ohr

Chadash runs and participates in events and programs in cities throughout North America.

 Rabbi Avraham Arieh & Rachel Trugman, Directors
Moshav Mevo Modiim, D.N. Hamercaz, Israel 73122
Tel: 972-8-926-5247
Fax: 972-8-926-5448
Email: trugman@netvision.net.il
Website: www.thetrugmans.com